D0898632

FOURTEEN CENTS & SEVEN GREEN APPLES

The Life and Times of Charles Bair

By Lee Rostad

Fourteen Cents & Seven Green Apples
THIRD EDITION

1992 Lee Rostad
All rights reserved
3rd Printing 1996
Printed and Bound in the United States of America

For Marguerite,
who first suggested
this book,
and for Alberta,
who helped make
it possible.

TABLE OF CONTENTS

INTRODUCTION

As my sister and I were growing up, we never thought of our father as a great man—he was just our Dad and we loved him. He always thought of our mother and us girls and wanted us to have the best of everything. But it was only after we were grown that we realized how special he was.

My earliest memories are at the house in Billings. I remember running to meet my father when he drove in from checking his sheep and riding the last half block to the house. I remember Dad buying wagonloads of watermelons to take to the Reservation. I remember the Indians who brought their horses to our house while they were in town. There were picnics with the Browns, the Reynolds, and other families.

My mother ("Muzzy") was a wonderful woman and a charming hostess, and Dad loved to have people around. When someone asked Senator Tom Carter what the Bairs' address was in town, he just said, "Follow the crowd, and you will find the Bair house."

After moving to Portland, we did not have our Dad with us as much, but he was always there for the special times, and he made it very special when we spent time in Montana with him. We still spent winters in California with him, and, eventually, moved to Montana for good.

Years later, we learned what marvelous things our Dad had accomplished with his sheep, oil, and land development. He worked all of his life, traveling thousands of miles a year to see for himself how his ventures were doing.

I am happy to share the memories of my Dad and my dear mother and sister. They are all very special to me.

Alberta Bair

Chapter 1
RAILROADING
The Early Years

There were fifty honorary pallbearers listed when Charlie Bair died in 1943—a reflection of a long life of friendships and achievements.

From Idaho a friend wrote, "...Montana will never seem the same to me now. I do not think that I ever knew a man who had such a host of friends as he. He will be greatly missed."

Montana had been Bair's home for sixty years. He had been the largest individual sheep grower on the North American continent with a flock of 300,000 sheep. He made a fortune in the Klondike Gold rush and had been a pioneer in Montana banking, oil, coal, irrigation, and ranching. He counted among his friends such luminaries as movie actors Bill Hart and Tom Mix; humorist Will Rogers; artists Henry Sharp and Charles Russell; photographer Edward Curtis; and presidents from Taft to Teddy Roosevelt.

Charlie Bair was twenty-six when he held the door rail of the railroad car, and with a graceful turn, stepped off the train as it pulled into Billings in 1883. He saw the town spread out away from the tracks in an array of wooden buildings and tents. Dust rose from the streets, hammers flew, and voices echoed from the tent saloons and dance halls. The promise of prosperity was in the air. Bair immediately loved the town and decided to be a part of it. His fortunes would grow apace with the fortunes of Billings, and he would share his success by donating generously to charities and ventures that would enhance the future city.

Billings would remain "his town" no matter where in the world he found himself doing business over the years.

Bair was a slight, handsome man with a ready smile and a full mustache that curled up at the ends. In spite of his slight build, he had huge appetites. He approached his ventures, and his adventures, with giant strokes, and when he was successful, that, too, was in a big way.

Charles Monroe Bair was born June 18, 1857, in Paris, Stark County, Ohio, son of William and Mary Ann (Unkifer)

Bair, both of Pennsylvania Dutch descent. His father was a farmer, and Charlie learned to work hard at an early age. He went to school until he was fifteen and then worked full time on the farm.

Following his father's death, Charlie's brother Alvin assumed the management of the farm and expected Charlie to do the work. Since Charlie considered this a lop-sided arrangement, they had words and Charlie decided to leave. He left Ohio in 1877, with fourteen cents and seven green apples in his pocket.

Charlie went to work on a farm in Jackson County, Michigan for $15 a month. William Brown was a good boss and Charlie worked hard. Since Brown's sons were not interested in the farm, he offered to leave the farm to Charlie if he would stay with him. However, after two years with Brown, nineteen-year-old Bair was ready to try something new, and he went to work as a brakeman for the Michigan Central Railroad. He was soon promoted to conductor.

Charlie in his conductor's uniform, about 1890.

In spite of his disagreement with his brother Alvin, Charlie stayed in touch with his family, and later when he began to make money, he sent some home to his mother to buy more land. He returned to visit over the years, although only once did he take his wife and daughters. Fifty years later as Charlie wound down his businesses, he would deed the land held in his name in Ohio to his brother. It was not Charlie's nature to withhold love and help because of an old quarrel.

Bair would say later that he heard Horace Greeley's admonition to "Go West" and so, in 1883, he did just that.

Long before the Civil War, Americans dreamed of a transcontinental railroad spanning the continent and linking the Mississippi Valley to the Pacific Coast, and in Montana, settlers hoped for a railroad through their region, thinking it would bring instant prosperity. Miners could bring in heavy equipment and have a way to haul ore out. Ranchers and farmers needed the railroad to reach markets.

Congress issued a charter for construction of the Northern Pacific Railroad in 1864 and granted the railroad the largest land grant in the history of American railroads.

Jay Cooke and Company, the great Philadelphia banking house, agreed to finance the railroad in 1870, and the railroad was built from Pacific Junction, Minnesota, to the Missouri River at Bismarck, Dakota Territory by 1873. However, Cooke had overextended himself so severely with the railroad construction that his bank failed, touching off a nationwide depression, the Panic of 1873.

Headquarters Hotel (Billings Depot) and Northern Pacific Railroad engine. Courtesy of the Montana Historical Society, Haynes Foundation Collection, Helena, Montana.

The Northern Pacific, reorganized under Frederick Billings, advanced out of Bismarck in 1879, and by 1881, construction crews were working along the Yellowstone River in western Montana Territory.

Henry Villard was the leader of a group interested in Portland, Oregon as the western terminus of the railroad rather than Tacoma and the Puget Sound. When they could not convince the Northern Pacific directors to change the western destination, Villard organized his so-called "Blind Pool," secretly raised eight million dollars, and purchased controlling stock in the railroad in one of the most spectacular moves in Wall Street history. Bair took a job with the Northern Pacific at the time it was pushing through southern Montana.

As the railroad moved west, the little town of Coulson—part of present day Billings in Montana—assumed it would be the site of the city the railroad would develop. Land prices began to soar; unfortunately, the Northern Pacific refused to pay the exorbitant prices and Coulson's plans to become a major city were doomed.

H.W. Rowley, a civil engineer with the railroad, was sent out by railroad officials in February of 1882 to look for a new townsite. Rowley located the new town at the east end of the Clark's Fork Bottom because at that point, there were two sections (deeded by the government to the railroad) that lay side by side instead of cornering. The new city was named Billings for Frederick Billings, the former president of the Northern Pacific Railroad.

With the arrival of the railroad, Billings soon became a thriving frontier town, and soon a street railway connected the new town with Coulson, two miles away. The fare of the horse-drawn tram cost "two bits" and included two glasses of beer at the Coulson Brewery. Understandably, the trip to Coulson became a specialty of the young men of Billings and their girls. However, by 1889, Coulson was deserted and the two faded yellow street cars rotted at the edge of town. The action had moved to Billings, which soon earned the name "Magic City," as hundreds flocked to the new town site. It would carry that name into the next century.

Charlie's town by 1884 had five hundred substantial buildings and a population of around 2,000 residents. There were schools, churches, newspapers, and over a hundred businessess providing hotels, stores, saloons, real estate, law officers, milliners, drug stores, photographers—anything needed to provide for the comfort and service of the citizens. The railroad built a large stockyard for the shipping of livestock to market. Charlie and a fellow conductor soon took advantage of the photographer to have their picture taken in their snappy conductors' uniforms.

Charlie met other young men in Billings who would play important roles in his life, including Peter Larson and Albert Babcock, who were elected aldermen when the city was incorporated, and O.F. Goddard, the Billings attorney for the Northern Pacific.

1883 street veiw of Billings. Courtesy of the Montana Historical Society, Haynes Foundation Collection, Helena, Montana.

Many stories were told of Bair's early days with the railroad in Montana.

On the sixty-mile run from Livingston to Gardiner, the out-going trip was usually on time, but the return trip depended greatly on how the fish were biting in Yankee Jim Canyon on the Yellowstone River. When bearings in the wheels overheated, they would "freeze" the wheel and prevent rotation—a situation called a "hot box." Hot boxes occurred frequently on the return trip, and it was necessary to stop the train. Bair, crew, and passengers would go fishing while the wheels cooled. Back in Livingston, Bair often took fish to his favorite eating establishment to compare with the other fishermen. He not only liked to fish, but he liked the competition of besting other fishermen—a trait he carried over to business.

Montana was still sparsely populated in the 1880's and trains passed by many lonesome ranches and homesteads, one of which featured a small boy who stood by the tracks every day to watch the trains pass. Charlie always waved and threw a piece of candy or small gift to the solitary figure. Many years later at a Montana picnic in California, a young man came up to Bair and told him, "You don't know me, Mr. Bair, but this red-handled knife you threw off the train for me on Christmas Day twenty years ago still recalls the pleasant memories of my childhood."

Others recall their parents telling them that when they didn't have the money to ride from their homes in eastern Montana to Billings, Charlie Bair let them ride for free. Children under twelve with their parents rode for free, but Bair extended the rule for children not accompanied by parents. On the shorter runs, Bair would fill the cars with children. The railroad complained of Bair's largesse on occasion, but the company chose to look the other way most of the time. As Bair explained, the train was going anyway, and the seats were empty. Charlie loved children, and he liked doing favors for them.

On the runs he made during the next four years, Bair watched the landscapes. He could see the country suitable to farm or ranch and took note of the water and grass. While still with the railroad, Charlie began to invest in land around Lavina, about fifty miles north of Billings. Here were gentle rolling hills with excellent grass—good sheep country.

First, however, Bair had unfinished business in the Midwest.

Chapter 2
EARLY ALLIANCES
Helena/Friendships/Statehood

Bair returned east in December of 1886 to claim the girl he'd left behind in Michigan. On Christmas Eve in Chicago, he married Mary Jacobs of St. John's, Michigan, a beautiful dark-haired girl with soft brown eyes.

The Northern Pacific had expanded to Helena in 1883, and Bair now worked out of that city, so it was to Helena rather than Billings that the Bairs went to make their home.

Mary Bair brought a large trunk which was, as she would tell her daughters many years later, only half-filled with a trousseau; she wanted to make a good impression with a big trunk. Despite her initial little subterfuge, Mary Bair was a warm, honest woman who never let the wealth and prestige of her husband change her basic kindness and simplicity. She would constantly charge her daughters to be careful of their use of money and not to let their wealth, or the wealth of others, impress them or determine their own actions and ideas. Although she enjoyed staying in her home, she was also comfortable traveling to Chicago with her friend Martha Moss to shop for clothes or going with the girls to New York.

She was an excellent wife for a man like Bair, providing the stability and warmth of a home life that made an anchor for the charging, enterprising businessman who was constantly on the move. Bair, in turn, wanted Mary protected and his home and family separated from his business world. He kept his business and his occasional liaisons separate from his family.

Those who knew Mary remarked not only on her good looks and charm, but on her delightful sense of humor—a good asset in the frontier of Montana.

By 1883, Montanans were working for statehood, a recognition that would make them a part of the country. With statehood, Montana would have full representation in Congress, have the power to tax local corporations, be given large grants of land to support education, and be able to vote for its own legislative and judicial leaders. Statehood would end the long procession of federally appointed "carpetbaggers" from

Washington. Too often, the territorial governor's job was a sinecure for out-of-work politicians and soldiers.

There was adequate reason to hope for statehood. The population had increased from a little over 38,000 in 1880 to over 132,000. Completion of the Northern Pacific added to the argument. States, not territories, had the power to tax the railroad.

A Constitutional Convention in 1884 drafted a constitution that was subsequently voted on and accepted by the electorate. However, the request for statehood was denied by the Congress; Montana had become a victim of national politics.

The Democrats controlled the Congress and the White House, but the Republicans were in control of the Senate. If a state was considered Democratic, Republicans would not allow it into the union. Democrats would also vote against a state they considered to be among the Republican ranks. The stalemate was broken in 1888 when the Republicans won control when lame-duck Democrats agreed to allow statehood to Republican Washington and to North and South Dakota. The Republicans agreed to a Democratic Montana. President Grover Cleveland signed the enabling act in February of 1889 which brought the Dakotas, Washington, and Montana into the union.

A second Constitutional Convention in 1889 presented a constitution that was overwhelmingly approved, and Montana was officially made a state on November 8, 1889. The fight over the permanent capitol was postponed.

The excitement of coming statehood and the bustle of a growing frontier town was exhilarating to Charlie Bair, and he wanted to be a part of that excitement, as evidenced by the location of the Bairs' first home at 6 Benton Street, just two blocks off the main throughfare of Last Chance Gulch. The Northern Pacific depot was located at the end of Helena Avenue, which was also downtown, although officials later decided to move those headquarters to the northeast corner of Lawrence and Cleveland.

Many interesting men and women had come to live in Helena to make their mark in the territory just turning to statehood. There were men like Charlie Bair—coming from humble beginnings in the East or Europe to make their lives. They were hard workers and innovaters who were willing to take the risks which might further their fortunes. It was natural for them to gravitate toward each other in friendship and business dealings. The friendships Bair made in Billings and Helena in those first days lasted all his life.

Many years later, when Bair and his daughter Alberta were in Missoula for a Woolgrowers' Convention, they called on the aging and ill Charles McLeod, one of the founders of the Missoula Mercantile. Delighted to see Bair, McLeod reminisced, "Well, you came in on the rails, Frank Bird [Montana Power Board Chairman] was climbing poles, Cook [A.B. Cook, noted rancher and breeder] started punching cows, I started in the store business, and we all made it!"

During the four years the Bairs lived in Helena, Charlie not only continued his railroad runs but put in for extra trips, should someone not show or need a replacement. He had decided that he would buy land in Montana and put his roots here, and with this goal in mind, his energy and ambition knew no bounds. He painted houses, mowed lawns—anything he could find.

On a more enterprising level, he noted that many of the railroad workers coming into town at the end of the week were too late to cash their checks at the banks. He started a check cashing service, charging two percent for the service. Bair was no fool—he carried a gun when he engaged in this enterprise.

While working on the railroad in Billings, Bair made friends with Peter Larson, whose success story became an inspiration to Bair. Larson had come from Denmark in 1868, with little money, no friends, and no knowledge of the language. In less than ten years, he owned a six-mule team and was freighting in North Dakota. As the Northern Pacific built west, he began handling sub-contracts and followed the railroad until by the time he reached Montana, he owned a "...whole county full of mules" according to his friends. In Bismarck, Larson met and married an attractive Irish girl, Margaret Moran. Margaret's four sisters also married railroad contractors: Fred Lamey, Patrick Welch, John Stewart, and Richard Porter. All of these men were later associated with Larson in contracting.

In the course of his work through Montana, Larson was awarded prime contracts and became the most important railroad contractor in the country. He was generous with his success, making many contributions to worthy causes. It was

Larson, along with Tom Cruse, who donated the land on which the Helena Cathedral was built.

By 1888, a year after the Bairs had arrived in Helena and five years after the Northern Pacific had come to Helena, Larson moved his headquarters from Billings to Helena. He and Margaret moved into a house at 812 N. Jackson and asked the Bairs to move in with them. It was a comfortable arrangement for both families. When Mary Bair became pregnant, Charlie didn't like leaving her alone when he was on the railroad. Larson, too, was away a lot, leaving Margaret alone. The house on Jackson looks much the same today. The two-story yellow wooden frame house built close to the street still retains the elaborate lattice-work trim on the eaves and on the front of the veranda, along with the characteristic low windows of the period.

The Larsons and Bairs soon moved to a larger home at 615 N. Ewing, where the Bairs' first daughter, Marguerite, was born July 1, 1889. Marguerite was named after Margaret Larson.

Over the years, the Bair family stayed in touch with Margaret Larson's sisters and their families although—with the exception of the Lameys—all had moved to other cities.

Years later, Richard Porter would comment to Alberta that the men had all started out together, but Charlie had made more money than the other four put together.

Still, the husbands of the Moran girls did well. The Welches bought the Davenport home in Spokane, at the time the only home in the city with an indoor swimming pool, and the Stewarts entertained the Prince of Wales in their Vancouver home on one of his American visits. At the time of Larson's death in 1907, his companies with Welch, Porter, and Stewart had railroad contracts in Alaska and on both the Canadian Pacific and Grand Trunk railroads. The three firms employed more than 30,000 men.

The Larsons followed railroad construction to Spokane, but later moved back to Helena and bought the Chessman home on Ewing in 1901. They had no children of their own, but adopted their niece, Mabel Lamey, who later married Charles B. Power, the son of Senator T.C. Power. Their daughters were Jane, who married Tom Tobin, and Margaret, who married the Earl of Carrick and lived in England. Jane continued to live in Helena until her death many years later, and the Bairs had the opportunity to visit her many times.

Other social contacts for Bair came through his affiliation with his lodges. Lodges formed an important foundation for furthering ambition among enterprising early settlers in Montana—the Masonic Lodge in many instances being the source of the Vigilante Committees in the early mining towns and later providing the arena for other endeavors to grow. Lodge members were the same men who provided the leadership in the community, the political circles, and the businesses.

Bair, who had joined the Ashlar Masonic Lodge in Billings in 1885, joined the Algeria Temple in Helena in 1888. Of the fifteen men who formed the Lodge the first year, most were the leading politicians, bankers and businessmen of the Territory. Bair's friend from Billings, A.B. Cook, was among them, as were Judge Himan Knowles, former governor B. Platt Carpenter, Cornelius Hedges, and T.H. Kleinschmidt.

Bair remained a faithful member of his lodges, and was later a signer of the petition for the Al Bedoo Shrine in Billings. In his later years, the Shrine Crippled Children's Hospital would become one of his favorite philanthropies.

On November 8, 1889, Montana became a state, and the mood of the state was in tune with Bair's. Statehood granted

Algeria Shrine members, Helena. Bair is in the back row, third from right.

more opportunities than territorial status, and Montanans were anxious to get ahead. Bair had a front row seat, watching the transition from territory to statehood, and sharing the

The Bair and Larson home on Ewing in Helena. Marguerite was born here.

excitement of the people. This transition also gave Charlie one of his first lessons in politics as he watched the politicians jockeying for position. Bair began his own political career by helping Thomas Carter defeat Martin Maginnis to become the first Congressman. His championship of Carter and loyalty to the Republican party was to be a continuing part of Bair's life. He learned, too, of the power and advantages of belonging to the inner circle of those in public office.

Bair's early contacts in Billings and Helena provided lifelong friendships and business contacts, but Charlie was ready, in 1891, to sever one tie in order to expand his horizons.

Chapter 3
THE LAVINA RANCH
Rattlesnakes and Turkeys

As early as 1884, Bair had filed a claim for 320 acres of desert land, which is now the site of Lavina, Montana. Lavina, named by an early settler for the daughter of a housekeeper, began as a trading post and stage station between Billings and Lewistown. A post office was established there in 1883.

The Desert Land Act, which followed the Homestead Act of 1862 by a few years, was of interest to Montana stockmen. It allowed 640 acres to anyone who would irrigate it within three years.

In October of 1888, Bair had paid $3000 ($18.75 an acre) for 160 acres about a mile south of Lavina, and, in 1890, he bought another 5,540 acres.

Bair had stocked the ranch with sheep and managed to keep working at both the ranch and the railroad. In April of 1890, The Billings Gazette reported, "Charlie Bair shed his Northern Pacific uniform for a few days and appeared in Billings yesterday in sheepherder's garb. He has gone out to the ranch to investigate the mysteries of lambing."

In 1891, Bair shed his railroad uniform for good and moved Mary and two-year-old Marguerite to the Lavina ranch. The two-room sod-roofed cabin and the frontier style of life were vastly different from the spacious home of the Larsons and the city life of Helena, rude though Helena life may have been by Eastern standards.

The Bairs worked hard, and Mary plunged into learning the art of being a ranch wife. She cooked for her family, the hired men, and any visitors who came along. In those days of wagon transportation, visitors might stay for several days.

One chilly fall morning, Mary started a fire in her wood stove to make breakfast, only to find a rattlesnake curled above the stove where it had crawled in through the sod to get warm. Mary retained her usual composure but hastened to find Charlie, who soon dispatched the unwelcome visitor. Mary then went about her business as a farm wife on the frontier.

The first year, Mary decided to raise turkeys to make some extra money. She killed and plucked them shortly before Christmas and sent them to Billings with Bair to sell when he went in on business.

On his arrival home, Mary inquired about whether the turkeys had "gone well." A chagrined Bair admitted that the turkeys had gone quite well—he had given most of them away to friends and to the needy. This charity was typical of Bair, his family would say later; he would often work long and hard at a business deal only to go around the corner and give his profit away to someone in need.

Winters blew across the low rolling hills of the Lavina area with a vengeance, but Charlie saw to it that his sheep were cared for regardless of weather. This regard for comfort and safety applied to numerous people as well. A band of cowboys out looking for strayed stock was caught in a blizzard near the Bair ranch one winter, and Charlie put them up and fed them until the storm abated. Years later at the Governor's mansion in Helena, Governor Roy Ayers was telling the story of the cowboys, and then he turned to Bair and said, "Charlie, that was one of the best things you ever did. I was one of those cowboys."

Still, things weren't moving fast enough on the Lavina Ranch to suit Bair. He wanted more. More than a sod house for his family. Household help for his wife. More for himself. He put the ranch up for sale in 1893.

The Lehfeldt family came on a visit to look at the ranch and decide whether to buy it. Charlie had neglected to tell Mary the reason for the visit, but when he came in with the wood one morning, whistling, she suspected something was up. She had never heard him whistle before.

Charlie had sold the ranch to the Lehfeldts, lock, stock, and barrel, even to Marguerite's handsome baby carriage, which Charlie had ordered from Chicago. The Lehfeldts remain on the property today and still run sheep.

Bair rarely discussed his business with Mary, then or later in their marriage. She was to be protected from the vicissitudes of Bair's business.

With the sale of the ranch, the Bairs gave up on "roughing it" and moved to Billings in 1893.

Chapter 4
BACK TO BILLINGS
Watermelons by the Wagonload

With his family successfully moved, Billings became the base from which he operated his sheep ranch and other enterprises.

Ranching in Montana in the 1890's had changed after the Great Blizzard of 1886, made famous by Charles M. Russell's watercolor, "Waiting for a Chinook." The country literally froze over, creating a hay shortage that killed thousands of cattle. Ranchers were forced to operate smaller, individual herds. The days of the open range had nearly disappeared. Charlie bought a small ranch of 500 acres out of Billings for hay and winter feed and leased land to run his sheep. It was cheaper for Bair to lease grazing ground than to own it, especially when the size of his operation fluctuated to fit economic trends. With this type of operation, he was able to use the money from the Lavina sale to expand rapidly with his sheep. Bair ran

RESIDENCE OF C. M. BAIR.

CHARLES M. BAIR.

One of the jovial men a person is always glad to meet is Charles M. Bair one of the stockbarons of Montana. He was born in Stark county, Ohio, June 18, 1857, where he spent his first eighteen years attending school and assist-

C. M. BAIR.

ing his father in the duties of the farm. The next four years were spent in Michigan, working on a farm. At this time Mr. Bair decided to go on the railroad, accepting a position on the Michigan Central. In four years he had risen to the position of conductor, but resigned and came

to Montana in 1883 and obtained a position with the Northern Pacific as passenger conductor, where for eight years he made the regular runs between Billings and Helena. Before leaving this position he had invested in a ranch and put his earnings into sheep and cattle. His growing interests here soon demanded his entire attention, and in 1891 he resigned his position on the railroad and devoted his entire time to the stock business, making Billings his home. In 1898 Mr. Bair sold his sheep, of which he had 25,000 head, and all his ranch interests, and invested in an invention of Louis E. Miller for ground-thawing in the frozen placer mines of the Klondyke. Mr. Bair made a trip to the Klondyke in 1898, taking with him 10 machines, which are now being successfully worked in the mines of that region. While in Alaska Mr. Bair invested in some rich mining property, which is now yielding him large returns. Eleven years ago Mr. Bair was married in Chicago to Miss Mary Jacoba, of Jackson City, Mich. They have two little girls, Marguerite, aged 8, and Alberta, 3 years. Their home, shown in the above engraving, located on Twenty-Eighth street and Third avenue, is one of the finest in the city. Fraternally Mr. Bair affiliates with the Masons, in which he is a shriner, and is also a member of the B. P. O. Elks and W. O. W. He disposed of his Klondyke interests this summer, again purchased sheep, and is now devoting his energies to the advancement of Billings and this section of the state. Mr. Bair possesses a comfortable fortune and enjoys it, is public-spirited and liberal and in every way is regarded as one of the leading men of the city which he has chosen as his home.

W. HANSORD.

W. Hansord, one of the leading flockmasters of this section, has been a resident of the state for the past twenty-nine years. He was born in Lincolnshire, England, and at the age of seven years came to America with his mother and sister, locating in Chadham, Canada. At the age of twelve years, following the life of a sailor until 1870, when he gave up the sea to come to Montana, locating in the Gallatin valley, seven miles from Bozeman. In the fall of 1877 he moved on the Yellowstone near Big Timber, where, with Mr. W. I. Shanks, he was engaged in the stock business, first handling cattle and later turning their attention

Newspaper article from the *Billings Gazette*.

between 10,000 and 40,000 sheep during the years between 1893 and 1898.

Charlie Bair returned to a Billings that had settled down from the hectic pace of a boom town. It was a city of running water, street lights, and brick schoolhouses. The Yegen Brothers store was valued as a million-dollar concern where one could buy anything. An opera house was built in 1895. Billings also had a thriving red light district and gambling houses. In 1898, the first hospital, St. Vincent's, was built, and the brewery began business in 1900. The Grand Hotel was the best hotel in town, and the Billings Social Club counted the city's leading citizens among its members. Irrigation was coming into the Yellowstone Valley.

Charlie moved his family to a two-story brick home downtown at 306 N. Broadway. The Bairs' second daughter, Alberta Monroe, named after Bair's friend Albert Babcock, was born there in 1895. This home would later become the site of the Fox Theater. When the Fox Theater was built in 1931, Mr. and Mrs. Charles Bair, Miss Marguerite Bair, and Miss Alberta Bair hosted a venison dinner for the Fox Theater officials. The deer had been shot by Alberta at the Bair ranch near Martinsdale. Following dinner, the members of the party attended the first performance of the new Fox Theater and later went dancing at the Persian Gardens. In 1987, some 94 years later, the site came full circle—the theater was renovated and re-named the Alberta Bair Theater of the Performing Arts in honor of Bair's younger daughter, Alberta.

The new Bair family home was a comfortable brick house with a yard enclosed by a picket fence. Family friend Carolyn Reynolds Reibeth recalled that the house "... faced east, and there was a small corner porch there, leading into the entrance hall, also small. But everybody used the side entrance, another, bigger porch, one step up from the sidewalk...In the north yard was a double-seated swing on which four kids could ride...I remember the bed of California poppies there along the porch....I remember three bedrooms upstairs, six rooms downstairs, plus halls and a big pantry.

"The cook had her quarters in the back of the house. In the back yard were the barn and carriage house and perhaps a shed or two—all painted to match the house (a sort of light gold color in my memory, and all looking very neat). Over one of those buildings, most likely the barn, were the quarters for John, the capable fellow who cared for and drove the high-stepping team, as he sat high on the box of the Victoria carriage, clad in a regular business suit and Stetson hat."

Carolyn also recalled early Billings in reference to the Bair home.

"There wasn't much pavement in Billings before 1910, and when the carriage went forth, it stuck to what little there was. There was perhaps five blocks of pavement around the B.P. Moss house (on what is Division Street now..."out in the sagebrush flats," scoffed some), and Montana Avenue was paved from the new depot west. I don't remember how far, but I do remember sitting on the depot steps watching workmen laying brick in the street. And I remember taking a fast ride in the carriage, sitting in the middle of the back seat between the two girls, as we sped up Montana Avenue and back, turning at the depot. It was dark, but strollers under the street lights seemed greatly interested in the strange sight of such a carriage. They were used to mountain wagons, one-horse buggies, surreys, and, not so long in the past, four-horse teams pulling covered wagons.

"Our Uncle Charles would not stand for dates, and boys hardly dared come near the house. Of course he couldn't prevent the girls making friends with the boys at school...Mr. Bair was a dictator in his family."

Bair's own team was kept in the stable behind the house, too, to take him to various places where he was running sheep. He always drove at a high clip.

A stranger watching Bair come up the street one evening raised the alarm of a "run-a-way" but the Billings native with him, said, "No, that's just Charlie Bair going home."

The team was finally replaced by a seven-passenger White Steamer car. Charlie sold Mary's team to Henry Childs, superintendent of Yellowstone Park.

The cook's name was Inga, who, in addition to cooking, took care of the flock of chickens in the back, so the family could have the traditional chicken dinner on Sunday. This flock never seemed to vary in size which prompted Bair to inquire of Inga the number and health of the chickens. It appeared that their neighbor to the south, the Methodist minister, did not have such good luck with his chickens, apparently losing one or two a week to the skunks. Bair straightened that situation out and promised the minister that the skunks (Inga) wouldn't be getting any more of his chickens.

Inga had a boy friend who came to call, and Marquerite would cut the yellow roses in the yard and meet him at the front gate to sell him a bouquet for his courting. It was a good business venture until Mary got wind of it.

It was a happy home, and the family was always close.

Charlie and friends on a hunting trip.

Although Charlie was busy making the rounds of his sheep camps, he found time to hunt and fish in the Pryor Mountains. His hunting friends were Billings businessmen W. L. Linton, B.P. Moss, and Harry Drum. Bair had special guns made for the elk and deer hunts, but he continuted to use his old fishing pole and worms and grasshoppers for bait. He remained a sportsman all his life and was pleased when the girls started hunting. On the girls' first deer hunt, he sent his men into the hills to bring the animals down a valley in front of the girls. When there was no shot, he went to investigate the problem. Alberta and Marguerite admitted that their first encounter with the big, brown eyes of the buck had stayed the hunt until it was too late to take a shot.

Charlie once tried golf, but by the time he had gotten to the fifth hole, he had lost all his balls and had started catching grasshoppers so he could go fishing.

Charlie at his favorite fishing hole on Pryor Creek.

While the Wright brothers were experimenting with their plane, Bair and his friend, Lee Simonsen of the Padlock Ranch, went to Kitty Hawk, North Carolina to see the flight. Charlie had an abiding interest in anything new and innovative, whether it was a personal interest or something to enhance his businesses. He was excited about the possibility of flight, although he found the car and train comfortable means of transportation. His only actual try at flying was a brief flight over Billings early in the century. Charlie also found time to continue his interest in the political scene, working for candidates and donating money.

Mary kept busy running the house and watching the girls. She loved to wash clothes, but Charlie did not want his wife doing the hard work of the household. When Bair would head for the reservation, Mary would wash clothes. Her friend, Mrs.

Babcock, would telephone from down the street when she saw Bair headed home, so Mary would have time to get the clothes off the line.

Artists traveled to the larger towns to teach, and Mary Bair took lessons in china painting. She was very professional, and her hand-painted dishes are a cherished part of the family home. Visitors came from the east, and the Bairs made many excursions to nearby Yellowstone Park or to Hunter Hot Springs during their Billings years. Mary Bair held Open House, a popular social event of the day. On the Fourth of July and other holidays, the yard was full of friends and guests enjoying a picnic. Flags flew and the exhilaration of the holiday filled the air.

One family photograph from the early 1900s shows the Bairs and friends on a picnic. Alberta and Marguerite wear flounced dresses with the obligatory lace-up boots and stockings of the period. They both wear pointed Mexican hats. A trim-looking Bair sits on the blanket while behind him, Mary paints a feminine picture, wearing a boater hat and a long dress that buttons up to the neck. The manner is relaxed, but the dress is formal. All of the men wear suits; both men and women wear hats.

The Bairs often enjoyed the holidays in grand style. The Billings Gazette in December of 1925, was headlined, "700 Children Enjoy Party."

"Seven hundred happy kiddies were the guests of Mr. and Mrs. C.M. Bair and their daughters, Misses Marguerite and Alberta, at a Christmas theater party tendered them at the Lyric theater Friday morning.

"Guests of the Bair family at the party included Billings newsboys, children of the St. Vincent's hospital school and boys and girls who by reason of circumstances, ordinarily fare less bountifully at Christmastide than their more fortunate fellows.

"As the kiddies entered the theater shortly after 10 o'clock they were greeted by Santa Claus who presented toys to each one. Their hosts supervised their seating and looked after their comfort during the entertainment which followed.

"A Hoot Gibson feature picture and an 'Our Gang' comedy were shown for the entertainment of the kiddies.

"It was a noisy, joyous throng that filled the theater, rattling toys, playing mouth harps and maintaining a din that all but drowned out the music with noise making devices.

"Susie was there, attentive to her little sister, and Bill tended his kid brother solicitiously to make sure that brother thoroughly enjoyed the party.

"For two hours the children enjoyed themselves as only kiddies can. Beaming faces bespoke their gratitude. They had a good time. For them the party added immensely to their enjoyment of Christmas. To the many grownups who witnessed arrival and departure of the happy throng there was little doubt of that."

Bair's charity was not limited to children. Charlie was particularly fond of buying watermelons by the wagonload to eat at picnics or to take to the Crow Indian Reservation. The Crow called him "Watermelon Charlie."

After Bair started running sheep on the reservation in 1901, the Crow would often bring their horses to the house on Broadway when they came to town and would leave them there until they were ready to head home. John took care of the horses, giving them plenty of oats so that they were lively for the next rider.

The neighborhood children soon learned they could ride the Crow horses, usually with Alberta in the lead. A run-a-way once took her all the way to the fairgrounds near the river before the pony stopped. When Mary went looking for her daughter, she found out at the livery station that Alberta had gone by, flat on the horse's back and hanging on for dear life, pleading "Help."

Like children everywhere, the little girls in Billings sent away for needles to sell in order to win a "talking machine"— another disappointment when the little machine only gave out two short phrases: "Uncle Josh on a bicycle, ha, ha, ha."

Bair was proud of his family and loved everyone dearly, but his second daughter was his favorite. Early on, he called Alberta his "Hot Toddy" when he needed a boost. The nickname "Toddy" stuck.

Marguerite was more quiet and retiring, as Mary was. She preferred to stand in the background and watch, but Alberta was her father's shadow. She would wait for his buggy and ride the last block home with him. When someone asked her name,

Alberta would would reply, "Don't you know? I'm Charlie Bair's little girl."

Charlie delighted in coaching Alberta on business. When she was about twelve, he gave her a house to rent on Twenty-Seventh Street. She drew a childish picture of a house with the caption "What a beautiful home" and put it in the window. She had to have a little help in the actual renting.

Early in the century, B.P. Moss, another Billings businessman, and Bair sent their families away for an Eastern vacation, starting at the Palmer House in Chicago, continuing with a tour of the Great Lakes, and ending in the Boston area. The husbands had reserved suites for their families, much to the distress of the ladies, who thought one or two rooms would be sufficient, a suite a waste of money.

The Moss and Bair children had a great time living in hotels, with permission to go to the dining room and order what they liked. Often, while Mary Bair and Martha Moss rested in their rooms, the children, Alberta and Marguerite, and Culley and Melville, would enjoy chocolate sundaes and crab salad for breakfast.

Marguerite and Alberta after a fishing trip in California.

There is no record of what the maitre d's thought of their guests from the Wild West.

Starting in the late 1890s, Charlie Bair took his family to California for the winter months. They went by rail to Portland where they often stayed a week or two before heading south. Bair and William Rea had invested in property around Portland, and the stop gave Charlie the opportunity to check on his investments.

In 1910, the Bair family was in Portland at the hotel when Joel M. Long, a former Montana resident, walked up to Bair and told him the rain was "getting to him"—he had to get back to Montana and the sunshine. Would Bair be interested in buying his home in Portland?

"Muzzy" and Marguerite in Portland.

In typical fashion, Bair bought the house fifteen minutes after looking at it, told his family, wired to Billings for his servants, and ordered his cars sent.

The house was newly built, a large twelve-room house typical of the turn of the century. A comfortable home, with lots of wood interiors and a large veranda, it served the family well. In 1937, when Bair sold the Portland home, he traded it for four lots across from the Midland Bank in Billings which he later sold to the bank.

Family friend, Carolyn Reynolds Reibeth, remembered:

"...and about 1910...he moved his women to Portland, where he bought them a nice house and a fine car and left them. He lived at the Northern Hotel, where they lived, too, for part of each year. Then Mr. Bair would have a big dinner for us all in the Northern's dining room."

It was typical of Bair to move his family without consulting them first. It was also typical of the family to accept this benign paternalism without question.

To Portland reporters, Bair explained, "For 27 years I have made my home in Montana. I have felt the necessity of giving my family some of the better opportunities of life, and for that reason I have chosen Portland as the place to live in. There is a tremendous future for Portland." He revealed his business sense, too. "You have the only water level city on the coast, and your territory is beyond question one of the largest in the country today remaining undeveloped. I have bought 16,000 acres in Yamhill County. William Rae, of Billings, is interested with me in this venture, and I understand that he also, is coming to Portland to live. He commands considerable capital and will take part in your progress, I have no doubt.

"I am delighted with your climate and I know that I am going to find it quite different here. Over in Montana we have some of the best friends to be found. There is no better state in the world than Montana, and it is with regret that we have decided to leave for the present and make our home here. The winters there are severe, however. We want to enjoy Portland's mild winters and take advantage of your schools for our children.

"We expect to do something with the 16,000 acres in Yamhill County, and I am inclined to believe that we shall experience first, to determine the best that circumstances will warrant. The Willamette Valley is the greatest in the world, and some day will be one of the most densely populated spots on the earth. I do not expect to follow any particular line of business here. I still have my Montana interests and that will keep me busy."

Bair shipped cattle to Oregon to sell. In 1913, his 1,400-pound steers brought about six cents a pound or about $85 a head in Portland. The animals were fed in Montana and shipped in ten cars.

Charlie was back in Montana in January of 1911 to take care of business and wrote to the ladies back in Portland that the weather was cold, 61 degrees below zero in Havre and 58 below in Glendive. He reported that the snow was halfway up the fence in their yard in Billings.

He continued "...I have met a great many of our Billings neighbors that say they will not stand for us moving to Portland. I console them by saying we only turned the key on the house here and may return at any time but they do not take to it kindly...but it looks quite old and dead and mighty cold here in comparison with Portland. They all say you made your money here and should stay and live it out here...when you have got it we can spend it where we like and that is all there is to it...have plenty of chances to rent the house but do not think it wise until we see how well you all like Portland."

Mary and the girls did, indeed, like Portland, and Mary's health was better. One of the reasons for the move had been Mary's respiratory problem: she had suffered from asthma from the time she'd come to Montana.

In Portland, friendships were renewed with the Porter family (Mrs. Porter was Margaret Larson's sister). Young Margaret ("Min") Porter was the same age as Alberta, and they became best friends.

Since the Bair family still spent much of the winter in California, Alberta did not go to high school but went several

Marguerite.

months out of the year to a tutor and music teacher with Margaret. Alberta professed to having little interest in music, but she became quite good on the piano. She felt in the shadow of her friend, who was an excellent musician. The two later roomed together at Bryn Mawr.

Margaret Porter married Robert Butler, who later became ambassador to Cuba and to Australia. In 1942, during a visit with Margaret, Alberta was able to participate in the christening of a frigate at the Butler shipyard in Duluth, Minnesota.

While still in Billings, the Bairs had taken the advice of Addie Sharp, artist Joseph Sharp's wife, and sent Marguerite to the Cincinnati Conservatory for voice and violin. She also

Alberta Bair as a debutante.

attended Anne Wright Seminary in Tacoma, Washington and graduated from Liberty College in Missouri.

While at Liberty, Marguerite met among others, the Heinz girls and Aubrey Black, who later married Richard Ringling of the Ringling Circus family and lived in White Sulphur Springs, Montana.

One of Marguerite's teachers remarked that it was too bad that she had money—if she had had to work, she could have had a brilliant career as a vocalist. Her performances were limited to local concerts, such as one given by the Billings Women's Club.

Marguerite's part was reported:

"The third number was two songs, 'May Morning,' by Denze and 'Spring Song' by Becker sung by Miss Bair, who possesses a fine voice, with much quality and power, and who gave her song with such taste that an encore was demanded and given. She gives much promise for a young artist."

The continuing education of the Bair girls in Portland included riding, shooting, cooking, bridge, and golf lessons. As part of her cooking lessons, Marguerite once made six butterscotch pies until she achieved what she considered excellence—then she never made another. Whatever the girls did, they did it well. In 1930, Alberta was the champion woman golfer at the Hilands Club in Billings; she later won the nine-hole club flag tourney, with Marguerite as the runner-up.

During World War I, Alberta was active in the Red Cross Association in Portland, serving as Commandant of the Motor Corps.

Charlie continued to spend a great deal of time in Montana taking care of his sheep and other interests. About this time the Northern Hotel in Billings became his second home, although he tried to spend as much time in Portland with his family as he could.

Northern Hotel, Billings. Courtesy of the Montana Historical Society, Haynes Foundation Collection, Helena, Montana.

The family spent summers in Billings and at the Martinsdale ranch, where they had rooms in the foreman's house, which was not a comfortable arrangement. One summer, Bair arrived at the ranch to find that his family hadn't been given its usual room, and worse, that they hadn't received the five-pound box of candy he'd left for them. The foreman left soon afterward. Bair would brook no disrespect of his family. Ultimately, the Northern Hotel was found to be more desirable, with conveniences, friends, and a social life.

Not incidentally, Bair remained a well known figure around the Northern Hotel. There were lady friends and a "social life" that was distinctly separated from his family. He often rented the second floor of the hotel for parties, some of which might last for days. When the family came, the dinners were sedate gatherings in the dining room. Although Mary and the girls undoubtedly knew, there was no diminution in their love and regard for Charlie. They accepted this as a part of Charles M. Bair.

Bair was remembered at the hotel as having a "good" appetite; he also frequented a little cafe operated by Frank Larson directly across Twenty-Eighth Street from the Northern. A lot of the bank employees also ate at Larson's Cafe. Larson sold them $5.50 meal tickets for $5.00 and if they were short of money between paydays, he would carry them until they were paid. Bair frequently went into the cafe's kitchen and sampled the goodies while he visited with Frank.

Bair's generosity was renowned. Pete Terrett worked as a bellhop when he went to college in Billings and saw Bair there many times. When Bair learned that Pete was a student, he gave him a $50 tip.

When Ellen Gibb first went to work for the telephone company, she put through a call for Charlie Bair. Not long afterwards, the supervisor come in and asked who had handled the call. Ellen asked what she'd done wrong.

"Nothing," the supervisor said. "Mr. Bair just sent over twenty-five dollars for you because you'd been so polite and efficient and had such a nice voice." As she approached her 90th birthday, Ellen still remembered her "tip" from Mr. Bair.

Bair was generous to his favorite paper boy, too. The boy was helping his mother support their family, and Bair paid him $1 for his paper each day, delivered in front of the Northern Hotel.

Years later, when the Bair family had dinner at the Brown Derby in Los Angeles, the owner, Bob Comp, refused to charge them. He had been that paper boy from Billings.

Chapter 5
BANKING
Down to Business

Bair became involved with banking as early as 1894, when (along with his friend A.L. Babcock) he was listed as a director of the Billings First National Bank.

The first bank in Billings was organized in 1886 by Edward Bailey and Parmley Billings, the oldest son of Frederick Billings. The name of the bank, Bailey and Billings, was changed after a couple of years to the Bank of Billings and was succeeded in 1891 by the Yellowstone National Bank. A.L. Babcock was the president of the Yellowstone National Bank, and both Bair and Peter Larson were listed as directors.

Banks first sprang up in Montana gold mining camps and towns to answer the need for credit facilities. The first bank in Montana Territory was a substantial stone building at Virginia City in 1864. With the advent of the Northern Pacific Railroad, new banks were founded in any sizeable town as the railroad moved west. Several were started in Billings.

With the leaders of the territory behind the banking business, there were few failures and a large percentage of successess. These banks provided the territory and state with credit to expand its businesses, beginning with the placer mining camps and continuing through the period of railroad development, mining development, and a sometimes volatile livestock industry. Bair's friend Babcock was one of these leaders.

Albert Babcock was originally from New York. As a young man, he worked first as a printer and then in a country store as a clerk. By the time he was 21, his savings, combined with the savings of a young friend, enabled him to go into business for himself.

In 1882 Babcock came to Billings and started a hardware store and tinshop. In ten years, the business grew until it was one of the largest wholesale hardware houses in the middle west. He started a flour mill in 1895, helped to build an opera house, organized the Billings Telephone Company, and founded the Yellowstone National Bank. Bair went to Babcock to help finance the Lavina ranch.

The Bair and Babcock families were close friends as well as business associates. "Aunt Babbie" Babcock would sound the alarm for Mary when Bair was headed home or when Alberta was out exploring Billings on her own. Charlie Bair worked hard behind the scenes to help his friend Albert in his political career.

Charlie Bair was successful in making money, but he was equally astute at keeping it. He forsaw the inheritance tax, and in 1913, he set up the Bair Company and made Mary and the girls stockholders. He gave the girls money to invest and guided their progress if they needed any advice, but there were no strings on their spending. In the 1920s, Bair sent $5,000 to Alberta at Bryn Mawr. When the college returned the money, saying that the girls were not allowed to have that much money, Bair insisted that she keep it. "That little girl is far away from home, and she might need that money," he told them.

Over the years Bair put property in the girls' names, and saw to it that the money made from these went to Marguerite's and Alberta's accounts.

By the time of his death he had transferred his fortune to his family, knowing it was in good hands. He often asked Alberta about investments or ventures, and sometimes they were both wrong. At one point in California, they discussed and decided not to invest in lands out of Los Angeles that later became rich oil fields.

Alberta once remarked to her father that he didn't talk very much. He replied that when he was talking, he wasn't learning anything. He thought business deals through before he began the negotiations. The girls later used the same techniques in their business dealings, and they made a good team. After agreeing upon business decisions, Marguerite would usually sit back and let Alberta do the negotiating, a job she did with great skill and tact.

During the years at the Martinsdale ranch after her father's death, Alberta consistently topped or equaled the market in lamb and wool sales and yearling contracts. The Rambouillet breeding made for fine wool and a premium price.

Another business practice the girls acquired from their father was to hold stocks. They were not traders, but investors in the stock market.

In 1910, when the First National Bank closed, P.B. Moss approached Bair and asked him to buy his home in Billings and the Northern Hotel. Bair's response was to offer to buy the Billings Gazette stock Moss owned. He explained to Alberta (who at fifteen thought owning a hotel would be fun) that Moss needed the home to raise his family and needed the hotel to make a living for them. Bair bought the paper stock and loaned money to Moss, later renewing the loan at two per cent interest to help him. He loaned money to later owners of the hotel, and one in Great Falls, as well. That, and the fact that he kept a room at the hotel, raised speculation that he was part owner of the hotel, although he never was. He always told "Toddy" that hotels and newspapers were the things to hold. He was also aware of the power of ownership in a paper. Aside from screening unfavorable publicity about the owners, it was a great political tool.

John E. Edwards of Forsyth and Gazette publisher Leon Shaw also owned stock in the paper, probably with money from the Anaconda Copper Company, which sought to control the state's media. During the many campaigns seeking control of Congressional seats, and the control of the Republican party in Montana in general, the Billings Gazette was solidly in back of the Carter faction. Its political alignment remained Republican as long as Bair owned his stock in the paper.

The Gazette stock paid no dividends at the time Bair acquired it, nor did it for many more years. Shaw kept saying they were trying to "accumulate a little capital."

Bair, however, continued to buy additional stock when it was available. Then in 1959, when the Lee Enterprises bought the paper, the stock began growing in value and in the 1980's, Alberta (the Bair Company) was one of the largest single shareholders of the Lee chain.

Kathryn Wright was a new reporter on the paper when Bair died. When she received the obituary, she went to the editor and said, "This isn't the usual way we write obituaries."

"This is Charlie Bair's obituary, and if that is the way the family wrote it and wants it, it goes in that way."

All stocks did not prove as valuable. There are a number of stocks in the files from the early part of the century: The Big

May Lode Mining Claim, Gulf Inland Oil, Monster Chief Mining Co., Emma Consolidated, Jerome Verde Copper Co., the Flynn Consolidated, and many others that never proved of any value.

Bair's custom was to use the banks of the area where he had financial involvement, although his primary banking was always done in Billings.

Bair's banking business from the days he ran sheep on the Crow Reservation and surrounding areas was done at Frank Heinrich's First National Bank at Hardin. Marguerite and Alberta also had accounts at the Hardin bank. A story goes that years later, when the bank looked as if it would fail, the girls wanted to take out their money. Charlie told the girls that if the Bairs took their money out, people would lose confidence and make a run on the bank. He persuaded them to support friend Heinrich, but it cost them the money they had in the bank when it did, indeed, close its doors. Bair offered to make the money up to the girls, but they declined. It was all family money anyway.

Bair was a loyal man, and he rewarded loyalty given to him. When he was cautioned to get rid of a foreman who was making too many mistakes, he said, "No, the man stays. What mistakes he makes, he makes with his head, not his heart." He was also willing to lose his money to remain loyal to his banker friends, as in the case of friend Heinrich.

When the Merchants National Bank was chartered in 1909, Bair was listed as a director. Bair also was listed as the vice-president of the Merchants Loan Co. which was affliated with the Merchants National Bank.

In 1921, the Yellowstone National Bank and the Merchants National Bank merged as the Yellowstone Merchants National Bank, described as the third largest bank in the state with resources of $4 million.

Bair was also involved with the Bank of Commerce in Forsyth with J.E. Edwards during the period when both Bair and Edwards were involved with Rosebud Land Development Company. He lost his money in this bank when it failed in 1923. Following World War I, a depression followed which saw the collapse of Montana agriculture, and the Forsyth bank was one of the victims.

The intensity of his loyalty to his friends cost him financially more than once.

Later, the Yellowstone National Bank would be changed to the Midland Bank in 1923, and then in 1929, it became part of a merger of seven Montana banks into the First Bank Stock Corp., a holding company that put together banks in Billings, Great Falls, Missoula, Butte, Helena, and Miles City. The First National Bank of Minneapolis and the First National Bank of St. Paul and banks in Minnesota and North Dakota were also a part of the merger.

Bair served as a director and stockholder of the bank through its various name changes until his death in 1943, a term of almost fifty years.

Bair was quoted in the Billings Gazette (August 23, 1929) as viewing the merger "...with especial satisfaction" because of what he termed a "vindication of the success of Montana's pioneering spirit which makes itself felt in business, agriculture, stock raising and finances as well as the government."

He would go on to say, "In the old days banking was more of a personal matter. A fellow patronized this or that early day banker because in most cases he knew him personally and knew it was a 100 per cent safe place to leave his money. To a large extent that condition has passed away. Nowadays we patronize the organization whose financial statement indicates its business acumen and strength. It was natural for the old style to die out."

He would probably think, too, of the time he stood outside the Midland Bank in Billings, puffing on his cigar, and assuring patrons coming to the bank that their money was safe, and yes, he was leaving his money there. Undoubtedly, he saved a run on the bank, but his daughters claimed he was "pea-green" from the cigar smoke when he returned to the Northern Hotel that evening.

Bair continued to be a large depositor at the Midland Bank. His savings and checking accounts were regularly in excess of $100,000 during the 1930s. Bair's personal bank books from the period show a beautiful script with each entry and withdrawal recorded and accurately balanced with each transaction.

Bair's habit was to stop in at the bank and get a substantial amount of dollars in silver or currency to take back with him to the ranch in Martinsdale. One of the bank employees recalled that Bair would always seem to go to the cage of a "new" teller.

Since he had been a director for years, the assumption was that he did this to see if the new teller recognized him.

One day, spotting a new teller, he presented him with a check for $100 and asked for cash. The teller called out in a voice loud enough for anyone at the officers' end of the lobby to hear, "Is Charles Bair's check for $100 good?"

The question was not answered, but there was a deathly silence, broken only by the hurried footsteps of Mr. Westbrook and others in authority at the scene. The teller wasn't at the bank long but later apparently had a successful career in the theatre.

It was through banking that Charlie made another life-long friend, Guil Reynolds. In 1895, Bair made a trip to Big Rapids, Michigan, and met Guil at a bank there. Charlie was impressed by the young man and offered him a job in Montana. On July 15, 1895, Bair met Guil at the Billings train station and took him to his home on Twenty-Eighth Street. The Bairs were awaiting Alberta's birth, so Charlie took Guil to the bank where the two spent the night on couches in the director's room.

The job at the bank that Guil Reynolds had come for wasn't yet vacant, so he spent the next month working for Bair on his ranches until he could go to work in the bank in the fall.

The Bairs took Reynolds into their home, and he became a member of the family. After he returned to Michigan the next spring and married Carrie Brown, the two continued to live with the Bairs, at their insistence, for another year. With the imminent birth of their first child, the Reynolds insisted on getting their own place. Both Mary and Charlie wept to see them leave.

The families remained close. Guil's younger sister was married in the Bair home in 1899. The Reynolds children, when younger, thought the Bair sisters were their real cousins. They were always Uncle Charles and Aunt Mary, and Uncle Guil and Aunt Carrie to the children. Carrie's parents, Judge Michael and Mary Alice Brown, moved to Billings from Michigan as well and became part of the Bair circle of friends. With a close circle of friends and his family well established, Bair, with his ever-roving appetite, was ready to venture farther afield.

Chapter 6
POLITICS

Eight Presidents—From McKinley to Roosevelt

At home in Montana, Charlie Bair was an astute politician, although he never ran for public office himself. He was acutely aware of the importance of politics in the life of Montana business at the turn of the century. Some wag once made the comment that Bair always seemed to be able to pick a winner, only to be told that often he supported both candidates. Bair had personally known every president from McKinley to Roosevelt.

Cartoon from Butte paper, the Democratic, in 1908. Edward Donlan lost the Governor's race to Edwin Norris.

The Democrats claimed that the Republican machine has "...at its command every Indian agent, every land officer and every forestry warden... Certain members of the ring have in a few years become sheep kings through the favoritism of the machine in securing grazing privileges on the Crow Indian reservation, and another distinquished citizen on the west side of the state, who is already designated as a lumber king is cutting timber upon the Flathead Indian reservation."

The politics of early Montana were interesting and complex. Many of the first settlers were "refugees" from the Civil War, and they brought their political beliefs along with their belongings.

Politics were also affected by the topography of the state with its mining and timber in the west, dryland farming in the east, and cattle and sheep operations in both. Early on, the Anaconda Copper Company and the Montana Power Company became major players in Montana politics, with Anaconda the dominant partner. The three trans-continental railroads were aligned with the "Montana Twins." A further dimension was added by the battle among the copper titans, William Andrews Clark, Marcus Daly, and F. Augustus Heinze. These men had an effect on Montana history for many years.

Both Clark and Daly were Democrats. When Clark decided to run as the territorial delegate to Congress in 1888, he was defeated by a young Republican, Thomas H. Carter. Clark perceived at once that Daly had thrown his support to Carter. Charlie Bair began working for Carter, becoming his campaign manager in Eastern Montana in subsequent election attempts.

This was not a case of personal animosity. Daly was involved with the Montana Improvement Company which had a contract with the Northern Pacific to supply timber, lumber, cordwood, and other lumber products from Miles City to the Walla Walla Junction, a distance of 925 miles. Without a survey, cutting had been done indiscriminately on railroad and public land right-of-way.

With the election of Grover Cleveland, both an honest man and a conservationist, and his appointment of William Sparks to the Commissioner of Public Lands, the Montana Improvement Company was sued for activities that were "depredations upon public timber (that) are universal, flagrant and limitless."

By 1888, the federal government's suits were still pending. Daly and the other officials of the MIC and the Northern Pacific were convinced that Harrison would be elected president and both houses would return Republican majorities. They believed that if Republican Carter were elected, he would be of assistance to them in the Republican controlled government, but if Clark went from Montana as a Democrat, he would be of little help in the administration.

Carter agreed to work to quash the indictments against the MIC in return for its support. He was as good as his word, and the indictments were withdrawn.

When Clark was finally elected to the Senate in 1899, he was forced by charges of bribery (brought by Daly) to resign. That same year, the Standard Oil Company purchased the Anaconda Company, becoming the Amalgamated Copper Company. Daly retired to New York, a sick man. Clark continued to battle Amalgamated with the help of a newcomer, F. Augustus Heinze.

Through various schemes, Heinze's tactics cost Amalgamated so much it closed down its operations in 1903, putting about four-fifths of the wage earners of the state out of work. Winter was coming on, and the state was completely paralyzed.

In October, Amalgamated lay down its terms. It wanted a special session of the legislature to pass a "Fair Trials Bill" permitting a change of venue if either party to a civil suit considered the judge corrupt or prejudiced. Heinze was effectively defeated and sold his Montana interests to Amalgamated for $10,000,000.

In 1915, the Amalgamated Copper Company dissolved itself as a holding company and the Anaconda Company took over once more. Standard Oil got out of the copper business. The "copper conflict" left a bitter legacy for Montana politics for many years.

When the Progressive movement of 1905-1913 reached Montana, the Republican party was in control with Senator Carter firmly in charge. In eastern Montana, Carter's friend, Charles Bair, remained aware of the use and business of politics.

Carter came to Montana in 1882, a year before Bair, and established himself as a lawyer in Helena. In 1891, he was appointed Commissioner of the General Land Office, and a year later became the chairman of the Republican National Committee. He was elected to the United States Congress in 1895 and served two non-consecutive terms as United States Senator. He served as president of the National Commission of the St. Louis World's Fair in 1902.

Even out of office, with a Republican president in the White House and Montana's representatives being Democratic, Carter was an important figure in Montana politics. He was a frequent guest of the Bairs, often staying at their home in Billings. On election day, the party gathered at the Bair house to await results. Oyster stew was traditional for this late supper event.

The Bair home was only a block from the business district in Billings, and Alberta was politically active early on as a dispenser of window placards to the stores and barber shops. Proprietors were happy to put the placards in the window, only to take them out again after she had gone. Alberta subsequently made a habit of going back to check on the windows.

Charlie made sure that all of his sheepherders voted. He would see that they had someone to watch the sheep while he rounded them up and brought them to town.

Carter, Bair, John Edwards of Forsyth, and Thomas Marlow of Helena formed a formidable political clique that was often at loggerheads with the Joseph M. Dixon faction of the Republican party. Dixon served in the Senate from 1907-1913 and as governor from 1920-1924.

Carter had been a political leader in the Republican party for a decade before Dixon was elected to the state legislature. Dixon and Carter, although members of the same party, differed in temperment and ideology. When Dixon failed to become a follower of Carter, it became obvious that their ambitions conflicted. The eastern Montana Republicans aligned with Carter, but the western Republicans followed Dixon.

Businessmen in Billings had been agitating for over a decade to have legislation that would open the Crow Reservation to white settlement. Western Montana businessmen were equally interested in opening the Flathead Reservation. In his first session in the House, Dixon introduced a bill to open the Crow Indian Reservation. Its passage delighted those in Billings. Many, like Bair, were Carter supporters. Then as a Senator in 1908, Dixon was sitting on the Committee for Indian Affairs at the time that hearings were held on the mismanagement of the Crow Reservation. This involvement with the Crow Reservation at the time Bair was running sheep there, made Dixon a reluctant ally of Bair.

The following Christmas, Bair sent Dixon a painting done by Sharp "...in appreciation for the manly and able manner in which you stood by us last winter." Bair sought Dixon's help over legislation on wool tariffs as well. Dixon wrote to Bair in May of 1909, thanking him for the Indian articles he had sent, although attributing most of the thanks from Mrs. Dixon, who was so "pleased to receive them"; he preferred to pass any sense of obligation on to Mrs. Dixon.

Even after Carter's death in 1911, the Carter faction continued to battle the Dixon faction for power and patronage in the state. Neither side was bashful about trying to embarrass the other, either by trying to expose some moral lapse or by asking for appointments that were unfavorable to those in the position of appointing. Bair worked behind the scenes, content to help elect his friends. By 1927, Guil Reynolds, J.F. Goddard, and Bair were "anxious to wipe out the stain" of working against Dixon, and they offered to help him win the Senate seat. Burton K. Wheeler was re-elected with a 12,470 margin over Dixon.

Bair also was involved with helping other politicians get elected, including Charles N. Pray, Congressman from 1907-1913, and a frequent guest in the Bair home. Pray was originally from New York but began practicing law in Fort Benton in 1892. He was prosecuting attorney for the twelfth judicial district from 1899 to 1907 when he was nominated as a Representative in Congress. After serving three terms, he was defeated and returned to Fort Benton to continue the practice of law.

Alberta also recalled that once her father was among those helping Granville Stuart in an 1886 campaign for the Territorial legislature. When Stuart was scheduled to make a speech, his supporters warned him not to mention Missourians. Stuart was active in the Vigilante movement in eastern Montana that dealt with rustling problems, and many of the rustlers had been from Missouri.

Apparently, he gave his supporters no assurance, for in his speech he concluded that not all Missourians were horse thieves, but all horse thieves were Missourians. In the pandemonium that followed, Stuart shrugged off the anger of his supporters, explaining that he didn't know when he'd ever get that many of the s.o.b.'s together again, and he could not pass up the opportunity. He lost the election.

In 1908, Bair served as a delegate to the Republican National Convention in Chicago, where William H. Taft was nominated as the Repbulican candidate for president.

Over the years, when national figures came to the state, Charlie Bair headed the welcome committee in Billings. When Theodore Roosevelt came to the state in 1918, Bair arranged a special dinner that was talked about in Billings for years. As a preliminary, cowboys and cowgirls put on a rodeo. Roosevelt said he had "...never seen 'em go so high or fall so hard." Then followed a dinner of lake trout, blue mountain grouse, and sage hens that made Mr. Roosevelt, upon arriving home, wire back his astonishment and appreciation of the entertainment and meal he had enjoyed. For Roosevelt's return East, Bair saw that the former president's private car was laden with a grand supply of the finest fish and game Montana could supply.

Secretary of Agriculture William Jardine visited the state in 1927 to campaign for Herbert Hoover. Jardine was given a dinner at the Northern Hotel where the menu included trout and canvasback duck brought by Bair from his Martinsdale ranch. The menu and Mr. Jardine's appreciation of the out-of-the-ordinary repast apparently was more newsworthy than the politician's statements, since news of the food was the only report in the newspapers regarding Jardine's visit.

The papers also recorded that when Major General James G. Harbord came to the state to accept on the government's behalf the land on the Crow Reservation tendered for park purposes by Chief Plenty Coups, he was entertained at the Hilands Club by Charlie and Alberta.

Later, when Secretary of Interior Dr. Hubert Work visited during Coolidge's administration to inspect the largest wheat field in the world at the Campbell corporation ranch near Hardin, Bair accompanied the secretary on his tour in his private railroad car.

Charlie was equally hospitable to all. Once, when Mary had taken Marguerite back East to enter school, Alberta found herself serving as hostess to Bair's guest for the evening, "someone important from Washington." The twelve-year old Alberta looked him over and inquired of her father if the guest were one of his sheepherders since Bair was entertaining him so grandly.

With Bair's near-legendary hospitality, it was often hard to tell whether the guest of honor was a president or a sheepherder.

Chapter 7

KLONDIKE FEVER

A Nugget For the President

In March of 1898, an item in the Billings Gazette reported all but one important fact: Bair had gotten "Klondike Fever."

"Charles Bair and Tom Linton returned this morning from their Seattle trip," the story began. Tom Linton had a clothing store in Billings, and the two families had spent part of the winter together in Southern California before the Seattle trip.

"They report the weather delightful on the coast, with flowers in full bloom and Klondikers ready to bud and blossom," the newspaper report continued. While in Seattle the two had met Phil Mercer, a Livingston restaurant man, who had operated a water wagon between the city and the river in Billings' early days. Three of Mercer's brothers had just returned from the Klondike, "bringing with them $60,000 in gold dust which they took from a trench less than 120 feet in length, and Phil was having a rattling good time. He took the Billings gentlemen out to see the sights, treated them to dandelion supper and threw money to the birds," the report concluded.

Bair didn't want to dig in the gold fields himself, although on the two trips he later made to the Yukon, he did in fact do just that. On his first trip, he examined the existing opportunities; obviously, he was impressed.

A gold strike on Bonanza Creek in Yukon Territory just east of the Alaskan border led to the Klondike stampede of 1897-1898. Some upwards of 30,000 prospectors stampeded the area by 1898, and Bair's competition was stiff. However, Bair had another angle. Again from the Gazette:

"C. M. Bair, the well known flockmaster of Billings, who has two or three bands of sheep in this country, is going to the Klondike, his 20,000 head of sheep now being for sale for $100,000. He has a scheme which there is undoubtedly millions of money, and associated with him in the enterprise are Thos. Linton of Billings, Mr. Seaman, a cattleman on the Mussellshell and well known Helena cattleman. Mr. Bair, who recently returned from a trip to Seattle, has a friend who has invented, patented and perfected a machine to thaw out frozen ground with hot water."

The Gazette went on to explain: "In the Kondike the placer mining is all done in frozen ground, which is thawed by building fires in the surface with wood that costs $60.00 a cord. Besides the heavy expenses, it takes about 30 days to thaw the ground to bedrock by this method." However, the new machine had demonstrated that it could do the work in a single day, consuming only about one-twentieth part of the fuel, the report said.

"Besides thawing the ground, it also washes the dirt as thoroughly as can be done by the strongest hydraulic pressure, and several Klondike miners who saw the test made in Seattle at once offered Mr. Bair an interest in exceedingly rich claims if he would put such a machine to work on them."

The Gazette then explained the men's plan: "The owner of the machine has gone into Klondike with it, Mr. Bair and his associates will make arrangements to have them manufactured in Seattle and Victoria and expect to have 20 or 30 of them in operation this year. It is surely a great proposition and Charlie Bair, who was always lucky, has probably struck it richer in this enterprise than any miner in the Klondike. He deserves his good luck, though, for he is a hard worker and a prince of good fellows."

Bair sold his sheep in May of 1898 and again left for the Yukon. Arriving in Skagway in southern Alaska, he took the difficult path over White Pass at Skagway to the gold fields. He was over forty years old and had added pounds to his once sparse figure, but he plunged into the gold rush with the same exuberance he had demonstrated with sheep ranching.

Most of the promising claims had been taken, but he bought a claim, #51 above Bonanza Creek near Dawson, which proved extremely successful.

As soon as the machines arrived (only ten were made), he sold them at at nice profit and bought interest in several good claims. As the summer ended, he gave his mules and gear to another man from Montana, who had suffered bad luck and was about ready to quit. Bair planned to leave before the fall freeze.

As he visited with the man from Montana, a third miner rushed up and inquired about boats to Dawson. His wife was ill and he needed to get her to a doctor immediately. The Montana miner visiting with Bair said he would take them at once. Bair and the miner with the sick wife jumped into the proffered boat and headed down the river.

Reaching Dawson, the miner thanked the boatman profusely and asked what he could pay him. The good samaritan shrugged it off, saying it wasn't his boat anyway. Bair hadn't intended to be a party to theft, but he was on his way home, by any means.

Bair returned to Montana a very rich man. He had parlayed his $100,000 from the sale of his sheep into over a million dollars. His partners in Billings were pleased with the venture, and one of them remarked that "...he is just the type for a trip like that [to the Yukon] and is probably selling snowballs to the Eskimos."

After arriving home, Bair left for the East to finalize patents and title on the thawing machine. He went first to Washington and called on his old boyhood friend, now the 25th President of the United States, William McKinley. Bair had known McKinley in Ohio, and the younger Bair had admired the returning Civil War veteran.

Bair had brought some nuggets from the Klondike, and taking a handful from his pocket, he asked the president to pick one. McKinley remarked, "Charlie, you handle those nuggets just like we handled shelled corn back in Ohio." The nugget the president selected was the one Bair had hoped he would pick, one flecked with blue quartz and later worn on the Presidential watch chain.

Bair had another nugget similar to the one he gave McKinley which he had made into a stick pin that became his trademark for the rest of his life. Questioned once about the advisability of wearing such an expensive piece all the time, his only remark was, "Where I go, the nugget goes."

Some of the youngsters in Billings benefited, too, from the pocketful of nuggets. Bair handed them out until they were gone.

With his very substantial "grubstake" from the Klondike, Bair was again ready to devote his considerable business acumen to Montana.

Chapter 8
SHEEP ON THE RESERVATION
Chief Plenty Coups and Helen Grey

When Bair returned from the Klondike, he went back into the sheep business, leasing land around Billings, Forsyth, the Hardin area, and part of the Crow Reservation. Many of his leases were with the Northern Pacific for railroad land.

By 1900 sheep in Montana numbered roughly six million head, making Montana the nation's number one wool-growing state.

Bair's friend, Guil Reynolds, after being told that he should try an outdoor job for health reasons, applied for the agent's job on the Crow Reservation.

The Billings Gazette reported in 1902: "Guil is known in municipal affairs and is serving as alderman for the second term from his ward. What he has been lacking in avoirdupois as an alderman he has made up in oratory and sharp repartee in debate. In the council, he has been the guiding star, the one man to who his colleagues looked to for wise council and advice. Outside the city affairs the appointee to the Crow Reservation has been unknown to state and county politics. His time has been largely devoted to business since coming to Montana several years ago."

Again from the Billings Gazette:

"The appointment of Mr. Reynolds came as a surprise to all the old line Republicans in the county. They had not the slightest intimation that he was even a candidate for the position. Naturally, when the announcement came that he was named as the chief medicine man and guardian of the Crows, Republicans who usually know what is going on in the councils of the party began to look around for the club which had knocked over the ropes.

"They gathered in small groups and discussed the matter, while Charley Bair perambulated up and down streets with a smile on his face that would lay in the shade the smiles he wore in the good old days when he used to help his friend Colonel Babcock into legislative offices in the county. Mr. Bair strolled into corners where he could not be observed in order to shake hands with himself. The event is worth 10 years in Mr. Bair's life. To catch the other fellows napping is a trick in politics that ought to make any man feel like congratulating himself. The coup places Mr. Bair at once as the chieftain of his party in this section, at least as far as the dispenser of plums to be passed around is concerned."

Bair's influence had grown.

Bair had held the lease on the Crow Revervation since 1900, formerly held by B.P. Moss. His lease was for Grazing District No. 4 for 25,000 head of sheep, at an annual rental of $2,610. The lease was to expire in 1906, and in 1905 the bids were advertised in the usual way for leasing the district.

Chief Plenty Coups was one of the last of the great Crow chiefs and a great friend of Charlie Bair's. Prior to the opening of the bids, the Chief protested the leasing of the area for cattle.

Alberta and Marguerite (on right) on the Crow Reservation with Plenty Coups (far left).

When the bids were opened, the highest bid belonged to John Murphy of Helena who bid $8,000 for the grazing of cattle. Bair had bid $7,000 for the grazing of sheep.

Plenty Coups, along with Big Shoulder and Frank Shively (acting as interpreter) went to Washington to make his protest, claiming that cattle would break the Indians' fences and damage their farm lands. He argued that cattle outfits wouldn't buy as much hay from the Indians as Bair did. Under his permit, Bair was required to buy all the surplus hay and other produce.

Sitting on the steps of the Capitol Building, the Crow representatives looked like a small flock of blackbirds in their regalia, but they got the job done for Bair. Charlie later acknowledged that it cost him "an extra steer or two." However, his far-sightedness paid off.

Bair displayed his thorough and methodical turn of mind when he wrote the Commissioner of Indian Affairs defending his bid:

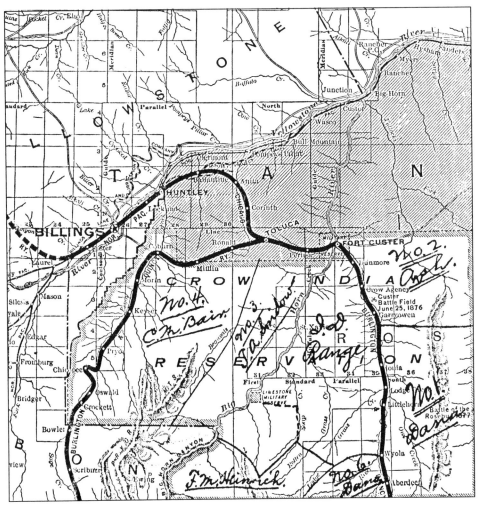

Map of the Crow Reservation lease areas, about 1907.

"Sir: I respectfully submit that my bid of $7,000 per annum for grazing privilege on the unallotted lands in district No. 4 of the Crow Indian Reservation in Montana is reasonable and the best bid from the stand-point of the Government and the Indians for the following reasons:

"First. Seven years' experience is an assurance to you that I will conduct myself in dealings with the Indians so as to avoid all trouble and insure peace and good will among them.

"Second. I will in the future, as in the past, purchase their hay, grain, and produce at fair and just prices and give the Indians the preference in doing such work as they can do with their teams, thus maintaining a home market for them to encourage their industrial advancement.

"Third. In paying them in the neighborhood of $10,000 a year for the produce of their farms and the work I give them, the income to the Indian allottees in district No. 4 is just that amount added to the substantial gain of the Indians over the amount which would issue from the hire of the district for grazing cattle or horses.

"Fourth. No crops could be raised by the Indians if the district should be stocked to its capacity with cattle, unless the allotments should be fenced in the most substantial way.

"Fifth. On my bid the Indians will directly and necessarily realize about $17,000 per year, while a cattle grazer would pay the pasturage bid and no more. Hay is not fed to range cattle in Montana, and even if the lessee agreed to buy the Indians' hay he would not be called upon to do so, because his cattle would eat the grass and the Indians would not have hay to deliver.

"Sixth. In addition to the usual bid, I have paid and will pay the Indians for the use of their allotments whenever and wherever used by me.

"Seventh. I have bought and will continue to buy not only hay raised by the Indians in district No. 4, but also east of the Big Horn under the big ditch.

"Eighth. In view of my seven years' satisfactory dealings with these Indians and their good will toward me, I feel fair rental, with an addition of my large purchases and the amounts paid for labor to the Indians, should be items subject to joint consideration in reaching a conclusion as to which is the best of a number of bids. To be frank, I say that, from a pure business point of view, my bid of $7,000 will yield the Indians more in rental and market than they would get out of double that rental and no market at home.

"Finally, I feel that I have bid as much and even more than the grazing is worth because of the cost of moving the hay which I bought from the Indians and now have left over. It would be a loss to me, would this left-over hay, and I took that into consideration in bidding, and ask you to consider my situation. Having by fair and liberal dealing gained the good will of the Indians, I have helped the Government in its work of elevating them. They are my friends and I am their friend. They are the most advanced in agriculture and thrift of any Indians on the reservation and I am proud of the help I have been to them, and now I put my $7,000 bid, $10,000 of annual payment to my Indian neighbors, and seven years of peaceful friendly relations with them and the Department into the balance, insisting that from any and every point of view my bid is the very best bid and as such is entitled to acceptance. Very respectfully,

"(signed) C.M. Bair"

Agent Reynolds, whom Bair had brought to Montana in the first place, also recommended renewing Bair's lease, and the Department of Indian Affairs agreed.

Bair was proud of his record with the Indians and their regard for his consideration of their problems. Of course, helping the Indians often added to Bair's own coffers, also.

Bair considered himself a friend of Plenty Coups and the Bair home today houses a magnificent Indian collection of game bags, beaded vests, moccasins, and many gifts from Plenty Coups. Plenty Coups' headdress and vest are a part of the collection.

One small beaded vest was a gift to Alberta, who wore the vest "...regardless of weather" and topped it off with a small Mexican sombrero her father had given her. Plenty Coups also gave her a toy tepee for her fifth birthday.

Photographs taken by Charles A. Benz during the early 1900's depict a visit by Marguerite and Alberta Bair to the Crow Reservation. Among the haphazard jumble of wagons, vehicles, tents, suitcases, bedrolls, washbasins, water cans, and dogs, these two fashionable and comely girls pose for the camera, wearing well-cut day dresses with turbanlike hats and high

Alberta on an Indian pony at Green's Ranch on Soap Creek, 1903.

heels. They seem at ease and almost playful beside their Crow friends who still sport the traditional Indian trademarks of hair braids and deerskin leggins, along with a more European way of dress that includes vests, shirts, pants, and dresses. Behind and above the figures loom rimrocks and the sagebrush-covered and scrub-dotted hills.

When Plenty Coups died in 1932, C.M. Bair was listed among the honorary pallbearers.

At this time Bair also owned land around Hardin about 45 miles east of Billings that he called the Alberta Ranch, which was later sold to the Northwestern Sugar Company, then to the Holly Sugar Company and which, in time, became part of the large Campbell wheat ranch.

Although Bair ran about 300,000 sheep at the peak of his career, he ran only 35,000 of those on the reservation, all wethers (castrated male sheep). His ewes were herded separately north of the Yellowstone River and on leased land from the Northern Pacific Railroad near Forsyth.

Bair's shearing sheds were located on Pryor Creek and on the Little Big Horn River by Garryowen on the reservation, and near Edgar and Huntley off the reservation. He was the second sheepman to use machine shearing (Thomas Snidow of Billings had been the first). In 1902, he sheared 9,000 by machine at Snidow's plant on Pryor Creek. He was an immediate convert.

"Not only is it done much quicker but also much more satisfactorily," he said. "A sheep shorn by a machine comes out of the operator's hands as slick and as clean as a race horse and there are none of the mutilations so common where the old way is employed. The animal does not look as though it had been run through a barbed wire fence or as if somebody had caught it and helped himself to a meal from the carcass."

Some of the hand shearers were not happy with the new machine, and Charlie heard rumbles of a strike. He immediately went to Butte and hired a couple of ex-pugilists whom he put in the shearing crew, and he got his shearing done without more incident.

From 1906 to 1908, Charlie sold 156,000 yearling wethers to Louis Swift and Company.

Other sheepmen using the reservation at that time were James Ash of Absarokee and Thomas Snidow of Billings (who was a partner of Moss). Stockmen who ran cattle were Edwin Dana of Slack, Wyoming, and F.M. Heinrich of Hardin.

Snidow bought some of the surplus hay and produce that Bair was required to buy, and the two often ran their sheep together to utilize the hay. During this time, Bair, along with one of his partners, William Rea of Forsyth, held a sheep drive that was the largest in Montana history. In the spring of 1906, the two moved 62,000 head out of Big Timber. More were added along the way, and by the time they reached Billings, the band reached 70,000.

The Billings Gazette reported that the two men had bought large numbers of sheep wagons and teams to make the big drive and expected to make about five miles a day. Half of the sheep were driven to Bair's ranges on Pryor Creek, and Rea took the others to Forsyth. A few days later, they moved 8,000 head out of the Lewistown area to the Pryor Creek country.

An older resident of Billings recalled that as a child he remembered awakening one morning to the sound of the sheep moving through the streets near his home. They were still going through when he went to bed that evening.

In 1909, Rae Bros. and C.M. Bair shipped 22 carloads of sheep to the market in Chicago. Eleven of the cars were loaded at Billings and the others at Park City. There were about 5,500 head in the shipment. Bair reported that they would ship another 150 cars.

Heinrich (known as Frank Henry on the reservation) ran cattle on the southern ranges while Bair leased on the reservation. He started running cattle in a small way in 1899, increasing his herd yearly until, by 1907, he had over 3,000 head on the reservation.

In March of 1906, Mrs. Helen Pierce Grey, who came to the reservation, told Guil Reynolds that she was from Collier's Weekly to get material for stories about the Crow Reservation. Reynolds gave her permission to visit the reservation.

Grey soon was stirring up the Indians, finding injustices that they hadn't recognized until Mrs. Grey pointed them out. Most of the charges stemmed from the manner in which the Indians were compensated for leasing their land, and their not being able to sell their livestock without the agent's permission. She also charged that Bair had gotten his lease fraudulently and that he ran more sheep than his lease called for. She charged Heinrich with running more cattle that his lease allowed. Grey accepted money from the Indians and went to Washington to personally petition President Roosevelt. Grey's complaints against Reynolds and the leases held by Bair and Heinrich led to a grand jury indictment against Grey for taking money from the Indians and a Congressional hearing about the management of the Crow Reservation.

In May of 1907, Z. Lewis Dalby, an Indian inspector, went to the reservation to investigate the charges made by Mrs. Grey.

However, Dalby found affairs to be "straight and proper" and with reference to Mrs. Grey found her to be "...not only an unprincipled, but a dangerous woman. If the spirit of these Indians had been a little different, I could not have controlled them as I did, and it would probably have been necessary...to call out the military to prevent an uprising. I have not at any time believed that this is imminent here, but I am convinced that Mrs. Grey would not hesitate to bring about such a condition if it were in her power and seemed to her to be to her advantage. There is but one safe place for her, and that is the penitentiary.

"I plan to start out on Monday or Tuesday," Dalby's report continues, "with Alexander Upshaw as interpreter and visit every district of the reservation. Without taking the Indians from their homes or from their work any more than absolutely necessary, I shall talk with all who have, or fancy they have, any grievances.

"I have gathered from a number of things Reynolds has said to me at different times, that as soon as this matter is settled so that he will be free to do so, he will resign. I have refrained from any comment at such times, as I shall of course recommend his dismissal if the facts developed in my investigation require such action. But my impression, so far as I have been able properly to form one, and my information from the most reliable sources, both white and Indian, is that Reynolds is the best agent that has ever been on this reservation. I believe that he accepted the position mainly or entirely because of the out-of-door life was what his health at that time required; that he came here with a laudable ambition to make things better on the reservation in many ways, and that he did actually make very great improvements, in which he took a very just pride...In my opinion it will be hard to find such a man who can afford to work for $1,800 a year, which is the salary of this agency."

As to Grey's complaint against Bair for running more sheep than his lease allowed, Grey told the Senate Committee on Indian Affairs that when she started to Washington in March of 1907, with a petition from the Indians to the president, "...Mr. Bair hurriedly trailed his sheep off the reservation...The Indians counted twenty-three bands (69,000 sheep) that crossed the bridge at Custer."

Reynolds explained that since it was the custom of the area to sell hay in the stack and bring the sheep to the hay and feed it near where it had been cut, many sheep probably were wintered on the reservation.

The arrangement with Bair was to bring his sheep on the reservation in the fall, winter them in the valleys while feeding the hay, and take them out again in the spring. He was to buy all the surplus hay from the Indians at a flat $5 a ton in the stack and pay any damages directly to the Indians for any damage done to their allotments by the sheep.

Reynolds further added that much of the hay had been put up poorly and was worthless. It was also eaten by the Indian stock, so much of the hay that Bair paid for he did not use. The Indians visiting at the sheep wagons at each meal probably increased the number to be fed several times over the normal amount but "...they were always welcomed and always fed without charge."

This seemed to satisfy the government regarding Grey's charges. Charlie had endured both the charges of running more sheep than his lease called for as well as personal attacks on him from Grey. ("He stole from the railroad. Everyone knows that.") He, along with the others accused, was relieved to have the episode over, and the reservation people went back to their normal business.

For Bair, this meant he was involved on a day-to-day basis with his sheep, a personal involvement that led to several adventures—and colorful stories.

Chapter 9
SHEEPISH TALES
More Sheep Dogs Than That

Bair's hands-on approach toward raising sheep gave rise to many stories in later years.

Bair constantly checked on his sheep, acting as his own manager rather than leaving it to someone else. He had an intuitive knowledge about how his sheep were doing, one of his hands once said. Sometimes Bair would hunt up a man and tell him to "...saddle up and leave on the lope and count my sheep." He was careful to take care of both his sheep and his herders.

Should a storm appear, Bair immediately took a train to Crow Agency and in his buffalo coat, beaver hat, woolen gloves, and buckled overshoes, he rode a saddle horse or team with sled to check on the sheep. He made a bulky picture with his winter gear, but he stayed warm.

Carolyn Reynolds Reibeth recalled later that Bair never came to the Agency without bringing a five-pound box of candy, specially made and packaged in Billings. She wrote to Mary Bair many years later recalling the candied violets and fake peanuts with candy shells.

Mike Reynolds, the oldest of the children, remembered "Uncle Charlie" as "...a giant of a man, indefatigable (sic), and absolutely fearless."

Years later he was lost in a blizzard, and the "pony with the rattlesnake legs" as Carrie Reynolds described Bair's mount, brought him safely into camp. By this time, he was a man in his fifties and weighed considerably more than in the days he was hopping on and off trains. That same year, he used two huge snowplows to clear range for the sheep to get them to hay.

Mike Reynolds related the rescue many years later: "One morning in January of 1903 Charles M. Bair came to Crow Agency from Billings on Burlington Train Number 42 and informed S.G. Reynolds, Agent of the Crow Indians, that 6,000 head of his sheep were snowed in on upper Tullock Creek and were without feed. If these sheep could be brought over the divide and down to the site where the Hostile Indians camped at the time of the Custer Battle plenty of hay awaited them."

Louis Ballou, the Agency carpenter, and Charlie Dillon, the blacksmith, worked twenty-four hours to build two snowplows. They were V-shaped and 16 feet long with an eight-foot spread at the open end. The points were reinforced with iron with six-inch straps along each side ending in a loop at the point where the doubletrees were placed. A wide brace bolted in four feet from the tip provided a place to stand for the driver.

The plows were loaded on wagons normally used to carry coal and wood. The wagon wheels were replaced with runners and the beds filled with hay and sacks of oats for the horses. A four horse team was hitched to each wagon. Bair and Reynolds rode in a spring wagon, dressed against the thirty-below weather in buffalo coats, muskrat caps, and eight-buckle overshoes. Four Indian policemen on horseback rode along to act as guides. They were dressed in wolfskin coats, deerskin pants, and beaver moccasins. Silk scarves were wrapped around their heads under their hats.

The guides—Big Medicine, Bear Claw, Sharp Nose, and Fire Bear—broke trail, crossing the Little Horn River, up the Cheyenne trail to the divide between the Little Horn River and the headwaters of Sarpy and Tullock Creeks. Bair and Reynolds followed, and then came the wagons with the plows.

At the top of the divide, the snowplows were unloaded and a four-horse team hitched to each plow. Guided by the Indians, the two plows continued down the Divide where the snow had reached a depth of three feet until they reached the head of Tullock Creek. One team would plow for a mile and then the other would take the lead; it was tough going and dark by the time the procession reached the sheepwagons and sheep.

At daybreak, the teams were split to pull the sheepwagons, and the procession started out: Bair and Reynolds in the lead, followed by the two plows, the sheepwagons, and finally the sheep, herded by the sheepherders and their dogs.

When they reached the divide, the plows were again hooked up with four horses and a trail plowed to the Medicine Trail crossing on the Little Big Horn River, where Custer had observed the Indian camp. The sheepwagons and other wagons were brought in later. Reynolds also reported that his father and Bair shot four wolves and three coyotes. The herders had already shot six wolves and ten coyotes that had threatened the sheep.

During the winter of 1910, the Billings Gazette reported bad news: "Last evening reports were in circulation throughout the city that Charles M. Bair, the well known sheep man, had become lost and had possibly perished in the severe storm that had been raging in this and adjoining counties for the last three days. The report was common street rumor..."

The rival newspaper, the Independent, in nearby Forsyth, retorted, "...the Billings papers are printing about two columns daily under the heading `C.M. Bair, the sheep magnate, is missing in the big storm.' Rats! and Rats again! Mr. Bair has been absent from Billings almost a week and because he hasn't reported daily to the hot air experts of that town this word goes out all over the country that eastern Montana storms are so severe that losses run in millions of dollars. The Billings self-styled boosters would do well to censor the newspaper correspondents in their town. Charlie Bair goes out prepared to weather any storm. He'll turn up all right, and when he does we trust he will interview the Billings papers and correspondents about their weather knocks as to this part of the state."

Such friendly rivalry between papers in their reporting of the news spiced up the long winter months for the readers.

The winter of 1910 continued to be a stormy and cold one, with many losses for the stockmen. In the spring of 1911, when a number of stockmen were discussing their losses at a gathering at the Northern Hotel in Billings, someone declared that Charlie Bair was lucky to have pulled through with so few losses.

Bair's friend, Judge O.F. Goddard, spoke up, "What do you mean, lucky? Charlie was out there plowing snow and hauling feed while you tender-headed amateurs sat by the stove."

Bair and his herders had indeed plowed out 78,000 head of sheep over fifty miles, moving them to better range. He had slept out at night, often in minus-thirty degree weather with only his buffalo coat, fur cap, and a blanket, with his overshoes wrapped in papers.

In good weather, Bair kept watch on his sheep, traveling in his buggy, and with his spirited teams usually managed to get back to Billings in the evening. Bill Huntington, an old-time cowboy who broke horses for Bair, told of a race he once had with him:

"Charley Bair was a great financier. His ability was outstanding in keeping his sheep and other numberous [sic] businessess going. He had quite a sense of humor. Bair enjoyed a good joke and always had a good joke to tell. He was a good sport. He always played the Billings Fair and liked any kind of rodeo.

"I was very well acquainted with him. I broke a bunch of horses for him. I took a bunch of sheep shearers over on Hay Creek and sheared out 7500 head of sheep for him.

"At that time there was only a few cars and the roads was so bad, and the country so rough, that he couldn't get around with a car. He had two teams of well-bred driving horses that he drove on a mountain-made light spring wagon called a buck board. And believe me, those horses could really get over the ground. He kept them well grained and he sure was proud of them drivers.

"I had a buckskin saddle mare that I used to run wild horses with. I was just like Bair, I was plenty proud of her. I don't know whether she had good breeding or not as I had bought her out of a bunch of range horses and broke her. She was fast, had lots of wind. I had done quite a lot of bragging on her.

"We was on Hay Creek at the sheep shearing plant about twenty-eight or thirty miles from Billings. Mr. Bair was going to Billings on some business, and I was going in, too, as I had been subpoenaed on a trial. I was going to ride Maud, the buckskin mare, pride of my heart. Bair was driving in, with his best driving team.

"He said, 'Bill, how would you like to have a race to Billings? I would like to show you the difference between a good driving team and a saddle horse.'

"The sheep shearers began to hurrah me. I hated to back down, then, I began to drum my head. So I said, 'For how much?'

"He said, 'Oh, fifty dollars, just to make it interesting.'

" 'O.K.' I said, 'the first one into Billings gets the dough.'

"His reply was, 'All right, we will make the finish at the Grand Hotel and no beefing.'

"It caused a lot of excitement among the sheep shearers and there was quite a lot of betting on the race.

"When we started I took the lead as Maud was nervous and wanted to go. I let her go because I didn't want her to fret charging around. I kept the lead for about a mile and half with Bair about two hundred yards behind. I knew that I was setting the pace too fast so when I came to a place where I could cut off a little, I took the short cut while Bair went around. I wanted him in the lead as it was pretty rough on the cut-off.

"When we got to Pryor Creek, he was a good half a mile ahead. Oh, Lord, how that team was going. I wouldn't have given a plug nickel for the chances of me winning that race. Maud wasn't showing any weaknesses, but I knew, at the speed we was going, that she could never hold out. I had a `hole card' that was pretty good.

"I knew when we struck Wet Creek that there was a cut-off of four or five miles. Bair would have to go about thirteeen miles while I would have to go about eight to the south bridge across the Yellowstone River. I would come in from the east of the bridge while he would come in from the west. He had to make the loop around Blue Creek.

"I figured we would not be too far apart as it was fast driving around the road for him. I couldn't make as fast a time as he could as I was going through rough country. I figured the race would have to be won from the bridge on into Billings.

"When I got to the bridge, Bair wasn't in sight. I was worried. I was wondering whether he had crossed the bridge or hadn't got there yet.

"As I was crossing the bridge, I saw a lot of dust flying. It was Bair coming around the dugway, about a half a mile away. How that team was coming.

"I didn't lose any more time. I was sure riding for town. I kept looking back. He was gaining on me. I was saving a little in Maud for the finish.

"I sure needed it. When we hit town, I could make the corners a little faster. I was giving Maud all she had. When I got to the Grand Hotel, Bair was just a block behind me.

"Bair would have beat me easy, but he got held up at the dugway as there was a bunch of sheep crossing the dugway when he got there. He couldn't get through them until the sheep was out of the way. It caused him fifteen or twenty minutes delay.

"Anyway, I got to the Grand Hotel first. That was the bet."

It was Huntington, too, that told of Bair's speed when he went to check the sheep. He was constantly traveling the forty miles from his home to his commissary on East Fork on the reservation. "If you saw a dust and something coming on the road like the devil on wheels, you knew it was Bair. You would just have time to say, `There comes Bair, and there he goes.' "

Huntington worked for Bair, shearing, breaking horses, and finding strays. Bair always paid well, he said, and he wanted a good job done.

Bair devoted attention not only to his sheep but also to his herders and others he employed. This generosity would surface again and again.

The Billings Gazette reported at Thanksgiving in 1908: "In keeping with his custom, C.M. Bair left this morning for a circuit of his sheep camps to make his annual distribution of turkeys, oysters, celery, and other delicacies which will be distributed among the various herders for their Thanksgiving dinner."

Bair could tell a good story, too. During the winter months in Billings, he and several of his cronies would gather to visit each day. A Helena paper, the Montana Daily Record, reported this story in December 1903:

"They were telling Christmas stories at the Billings club, and Charlie Bair, the well-known sheepman, was the only one of the party who had not contributed. The reporter said Mr. Bair is a capital story teller, but, he happened to be out of Christmas tales that year.

" 'We always have a Christmas tree at my home,' Bair said, 'but out on the range Christmas is about the same as any other day. I'll tell you a Thanksgiving story, however, and that ought to do just as well.

" 'It has been my custom for many years to give all my men a fine Thanksgiving dinner. Every herder gets a turkey on that day and other things suitable to make a complete dinner. This year the old program was carried out. I got a lot of turkeys and they were cooked up at home in the best style possible. The birds, with the accessories of a Thanksgiving dinner, were then sent to the range for the men.

" 'Among the herders is a fellow called Jim. He is a good

herder, understands sheep thoroughly, but he had his peculiarities. Jim thinks it not worth while half of the time to cook his food. The herders, as you all know, live out on the range in wagons. Each wagon is provided with a little cook stove, a bunk in one end, and various lockers in which to keep things. It is a little house on wheels, and in severe weather the herder can make himself as comfortable there as if he were at the home ranch. These wagons are hauled about from place to place, and are sometimes stationed at one spot for several weeks. It is just according to the range, you know, as the sheep are driven out from the wagon each morning and returned to camp in the evening. Now Jim, as I said, about half the time does not take the trouble to cook his food. He will eat his canned stuff raw, and some of the time he does not take the trouble to cook his meats. I merely mention this to show that Jim isn't an epicure, and the eating with Jim is merely an incident. Jim doesn't live to eat.

" 'On last Thanksgiving the camp tender distributed the turkeys among the herders. He drove up to Jim out on the range, and asked him where he should leave the turkey and other things. Jim told him to lock them up in a compartment in the wagon. He also gave him implicit (sic) directions as to where to leave the key. The camp tender did as directed. He locked up the turkey and other things as told by Jim and then moved on to the next sheep camp.

" 'That evening Jim got back rather late to camp. He started to get his turkey, but for the life of him he couldn't remember where the key had been hidden. He searched for a few minutes, and then, growing angry, flung himself into his bed and went to sleep. He rolled into the bunk with his boots on, never stopping to take a bite to eat nor remove his clothes.

" 'Some time before daylight, the little clock above Jim's head went off. The noisy bell hadn't got through ringing before Jim had piled out of his bed. He was still in bad humor, and, never stopping to take any breakfast, he hiked off with his sheep. He had no lunch at noon and by evening he was as empty as a base drum.

" 'That evening as Jim was driving the band into camp, he suddenly remembered where he had told the camp tender to put that key. As soon as the sheep had been rounded up on the bedding ground, Jim found his key without trouble. He was famished, and he prepared to have a big dinner. On this occasion Jim built up a fire and warmed up his turkey—a ten pound gobbler—which had been roasted and which only needed a few minutes in an oven to be in prime condition. Included in the layout were a can of oysters, a big dish of cranberry sauce, sweet potatoes, celery, and a mince pie. Incidentally, the gobbler was stuffed with oysters. Jim spread out the entire feast on the table before him.

" 'Well, you may not believe it, but the fact is that Jim ate that turkey, and dressing, ate his sweet potatoes, his cranberry sauce and his can of oysters, and then wound up with the mince pie. When he go through, he was stuffed as tight as a cow that has been six hours in a clover patch.

" 'We don't know how Jim spent the night. He got through it some way and left as usual with his sheep. About noon the camp tender got around the band, but he couldn't see Jim. At length, some distance away, he saw the man lying across a hump thrown up by a badger. He thought Jim was dead, and he hurried over to him. The herder was not dead, but he was in a bad way. He fairly writhed in agony.

"What's the matter, Jim?" anxiously inquired the camp tender.

"O, I'm sick, terribly sick, and am going to die," groaned Jim. *"Hustle back to the agency and get me some medicine."*

"They have three kinds of medicine over there," he said. *"Now, what kind do you want?"*

"Bring me a bottle of each," groaned Jim.

" 'The camp tender hurried to the agency as fast as he could. When he returned Jim was still suffering. Included among the medicines brought back by the camp tender was a bottle of extra strong pills. Jim eagerly seized upon this bottle. Yanking out the cork, the distressed sheepherder put a big handful in his mouth and then crowded them down his throat with snow.

" 'Jim is still alive, but he really had a pretty close call.' "

Bair could tell a good story, but often the tables were turned. He was the subject of many anecdotes.

A story appeared in the Saturday Evening Post some years after an actual incident in the nation's capitol. Bair was attending a dinner at the Washington home of James Hill, the builder of the Great Northern Railway and was introduced to a Washington lawyer, James C. Hooe, who had bought a farm in his home town of Bluemont, Virginia. That farm was the pride and joy of his life. Hooe inquired as to Mr. Bair's business and when told that he raised sheep, was quick to volunteer that he, too, had a flock of about 150 on his farm.

"And how many do you have?" inquired Hooe.

"Well," said Bair, "I haven't counted them lately, but I've got more sheep dogs than that."

When Grace Stone Coates was re-telling the story to James Rankin, she added this:

"[When Bair heard the question]...Bair turned on his heel, and answered over his shoulder (and that has the earmarks of truth; he was a N.P. brakeman, then conductor—and did you ever know a brakeman who didn't begin to walk away as soon as you asked him a question - and answer over his shoulder?)...The story was not a source of embarrassment to any of the family. Now you have the setting."

William R. Allen, Lieutenant Governor of Montana from 1908 to 1913, and a good political friend of Bair's, told this story:

"I was in Washington and met Mr. Bair who was there on business. We arranged to make the trip to Chicago together. Arriving in Chicago, Charlie remarked to me that he intended to buy a White Steamer automobile that would cost about $5,000 and he would have to cash a check.

"I told him I was going to one of the banks and would be glad to have him go with me as I knew that they would be glad to cash a check for him. The president, vice-president, and another officer of the bank had visited with me at my summer home in Montana. I had done lots of business and knew many people in the bank. On our arrival we were taken into the directors' room where we met the bank's officials. I had introduced Mr. Bair to them but they did not pay much attention to him, addressing all their conversation to me. While Bair was a fine looking fellow, he was dressed as a typical rancher. Finally, I said to the president, 'Mr. Bair wants to cash a check.'

" 'All right. By the way, what business are you in , Mr. Bair?'

" 'The sheep business,' Mr. Bair replied.

"The president inquired, 'How many sheep do you have?'

"Bair replied, 'Not so many now. I got scared about the tariff on wool that Wilson is talking about lowering.'

"This did not answer the banker's question, so he asked again, 'How many have you now?'

"C.M. said, 'About 125,000 head.'

"The banker said, 'For God's sake, how many did you have before you sold?'

" 'About 300,000.' "

Needless to say, Allen went on to relate, Bair got his $5,000 and could have had $50,000 if he had wanted it.

With his first big wool check, Bair and some of his friends decided to have a little fun. The Billings Gazette dutifully reported on the course of the practical joke:

"Yesterday afternoon C.M. Bair and a party of friends had considerable amusement with several of the cigar stores and thirst quenching parlors scattered throughout the city. The party, which consisted of three or four, would stroll into a place, line up in a regular style and at the request of Mr. Bair would ask for what they desired. When all were satisfied, Mr. Bair would ask for the bill and when told the amount would produce from his pocket a small piece of paper and carefully laying it on the counter, would say in a matter of fact way, that he would take the change in silver. The small piece of paper was a draft on a big Boston bank and called for $75,000. In all cases the clark (sic) would look at the amount for a moment or two and then with a gasp would say that it was impossible for them to cash the check at present.

"The party strolled down Montana Avenue and visited several of the well known resorts...One of the party finally suggested that they visit the Billings Club and work the same tactics there. It was agreeable and the bunch started for the cool rooms of that pleasant place. In the meantime some one had telephoned to Steward Tschudy and the bunch of live ones were met at the door by that gentleman. He invited them in with a glad smile and a warm handshake all around after they had exchanged the usual remarks about the warm weather, someone suggested that it 'was about time.' Tschudy was equal to the occasion and requested that they show something tangible in the way of silver, giving as his reason that he was short of small change on account of cashing several large checks during the day and that he wanted to stock up again...It was at that time that the faces of several began to wrinkle in amusement and then the party adjourned to a small room where cooling drinks were served by an obliging attendant."

It was the same marvelous sense of humor that made the visit of French Ambassador and Mrs. Jean J. Jesserand to Montana one of their most memorable. The Jesserands arrived in Billings for a one-day stopover en route from San Francisco to Washington and were to be shown something of the country and its resources and industries. The program called for a party consisting of the Jesserands, Mr. and Mrs. C.M. Bair, Mrs. Hahn, Mr. and Mrs. George Colby, Major and Mrs. S. G. Reynolds, Fred H. Hathhorn and Edward S. Curtis to go by car to the shearing pens at Kaiser where Bair's sheep were being sheared. They were then to go to Pryor so that the guests could learn something about the Indians. After lunching at the Donovan Ranch and watching the shearing operation, the group continued to Pryor, unaware that Bair had arranged a rather special reception.

Two hundred Indians in full war paint and regalia, filling the air with war whoops and gun fire, descended upon the cars and surrounded them. As the Indians circled the cars—a tremendous show!—Bair beamed with satisfaction and turned to accept the reactions of his guests, only to find them panic-stricken on the floor of the car. They recovered enough to enjoy the hospitality of the tribe.

When Jesserand was asked years later what his most

A train load of Bair's wool.

memorable experience had been as ambassador, he recounted his day on the Crow Reservation.

The height of Bair's career as a sheepman must have been in 1910, when he shipped a trainload (47 cars) of wool to Boston. It took ten days to bale the shipment of 1,500,000 pounds of wool for which he received 24 5/8 cents a pound. The train was labeled from engines to caboose in letters nearly three feet long proclaiming it "the largest wool clip grown by one individual on the North American continent."

In 1913, Bair shipped wool to J. Silberman and Sons in Chicago which was estimated at between 300,000 and 400,000 pounds.

The only rival to Bair's title as the largest individual sheepman lived in Australia, and there was some doubt as to who had the larger flock.

Chapter 10
BIG CARS AND FAST CARS
The Whistling Billy

Charlie Bair was as competitive in his hobbies as in business. He had race horses when the family first lived in Billings and sent them around the state for races. As he turned to cars in his business, he also turned to cars for racing. Bair liked both fast cars and fast horses, but he drove the horses and left the driving of cars to others.

Marguerite in "Whistling Billy"

An article in the Butte Miner in 1918 is typical of the spirit of the sport in those early days:

"Defying time and space, 'Jimmie' Reynolds of Boulder shattered all former Montana road records yesterday afternoon, when he hurled his racing car across 78 miles of mountainous highways in one hour and 29 minutes. Reynolds drove from Boulder to Whitehall and the 'Eighteen-Mile' hill to win a $1,000 wager from A.C. Snider of Spokane.

"Sixty seconds before the designated time—one hour and 30 minutes—elapsed, Reynolds' car thundered up Wyoming street, skidded onto East Broadway and slid to a standstill in front of the Finlen Hotel.

"Reynolds drove a six cylinder Hudson super-six. The car is a stock model with racing body especially designed for his needs. He was accompanied from Boulder by his mechanician [sic], Stiles Slossen.

"Fences, mudholes and fence posts proved no obstacle to Reynolds, for he crashed through all of them. In the Jefferson valley, near Whitehall, the Hudson struck a mud hole caused by an irrigating ditch. It skidded from the road, through a barbed-wire fence. Without decreasing speed, Reynolds dashed back through the fence, tearing down posts as easily as if they were but toothpicks. Tire trouble and a broken radiator took 15 minutes from the running time. When Reynolds realized that his engine was heating because of lack of water, the mechanician pumped oil and the last 10 miles negotiated with a motor which was literally 'air-cooled.'

"According to the mechanician, a speed of 95 miles an hour was attained at times."

Bair took delivery of a White Steamer automobile in 1906 (the third one in the state), and he got behind the wheel and put it into motion. When the car refused the command, "Whoa, Whoa," he clambered out and turned the wheel over to his driver. The company had sent a man to teach Bair to drive the car, but Bair kept the man in Montana to drive for him. He paid him $150 a month, a big price in those days.

Bair tried another time to learn to drive and attempted to ford a creek that was in his way. The driver said he didn't think Bair should try going through the creek. Bair tried anyway, and stuck the car. He left the driving to hired drivers after that.

Bair's drivers were always encouraged to "...go faster, go faster." It was also necessary for a driver to be able to inhale considerable smoke, since Charlie always had a large cigar lit up.

Bair once made the trip from the head of the Hardin Canal to Billings, a distance of 58 miles, in one hour and fifty minutes. It took the Burlington train two hours and eight minutes to cover the same distance.

The year after the White Steamer was delivered, Bair bought a race car—the famed Whistling Billy.

Bair had heard that his long-time rival in horse racing, mining capitalist William Morris of Butte, was negotiating with an Eastern firm for a racing car. Morris had the edge on Bair with horse racing, so Bair was anxious to beat him at auto racing.

The White Company was not particularly anxious to part with Webb Jay's famous race car, but Bair told them to set a figure on the car and he would pay any amount. Jay was one of the most famous racers of the time. Bair also left an order for three White steam cars, two touring and one runabout.

Morris appeared at the Chicago showroom shortly after Bair departed and said that if Bair's price was not high enough, he would buy the car himself. But Bair had beat him to it.

The car was a torpedo shape weighing 1900 pounds, with an engine "between 70 and 80 horse," and was said to cover a mile in less than a minute.

Bair raced the car all over the state, wherever races were held, setting a new record in Helena for five miles on a flat circular track at 4.54 minutes, or about 60 mph. On a good road, Bair could achieve about

Marguerite (foreground) and Alberta.

Marguerite in the family touring car, ready for a parade.

that speed in his touring car, but good roads were rare.

The Billings Gazette reported in October of 1907 that "Whistling Billy" would be a contender in the five-mile world championship race at Kansas City. Driven by Ralph Baker, it won the valuable Post Cup in that race, breaking the record set by Barney Oldfield.

In November of 1908, it was sent to Los Angeles for a race there, matched against a machine driven by Barney Oldfield. It is disappointing to read in a December 26, 1908 issue that Whistling Billy was wrecked:

"One of the most spectacular accidents ever occurring in American automobile racing happened at Ascot Park [Los Angeles] this afternoon when the front tire on the White racer, Whistling Billy, broke on a curve while Gus Seyfried, of San Francisco, was driving it at more than a mile a minute, the car turning three somersaults in the air, a blazing ball of flame and landing a broken wreck in the center of the track where it was practically consumed by flames."

No account was given of the driver's condition.

Bair had another "Billy" built by the White Company, classed as the speediest car ever driven in this country. He sent the new racing car on the road, winning races in Kansas City, Los Angeles, and Seattle.

In January of 1910, the car was returned to Billings from Seattle after a successful tour in the west. It was to be given a new coat of paint and stored in Billings for the winter months. Bair announced, "Billy has taken 29 races since the car left Billings a little over a year ago and as it has been entered in just 29 events it is returning to Billings with a clean record. The car is just about as fast a thing on wheels as there is in the country. It made a clean sweep of the records on the Pacific Coast and beat machines propelled by Barney Oldfield and Strang. I am told that in one place 45,000 people paid to see a race between my car, driven by Dundee and Seyfried, two San Francisco autoists, and a car driven by Oldfield."

Bair continued to buy White cars for himself and his family.

In December of 1911, Bair and William Rea made a business trip to Mexico, going by way of Chicago and St. Louis, planning to stop at his old home in Ohio on the return trip. Bair spent a day in Chicago looking for "auto" coats for the girls.

Writing to Marguerite, he reported, "I could not get as nice a coat as I thought you girls deserved so early this morning before leaving Chicago I started out again and ordered you a white auto to match the coat you have. It will be made to order especially for you ... the Dearest Marguerite in all the world it will be equiped with electric lights self starting and ...tire torpedo drive and the nicest thing the White Co can turn out. But they are afraid they may not be able to get it to Portland for Xmas as this something of the very latest style and am sure it will suit as it is a very classy racey looking car."

Marguerite had an accident with the new car, breaking her arm and injuring her father's knee. She did not share his passion for cars, but Alberta did, and she became the driver for the family on social occasions.

Several photographs from the family's years in Portland show Alberta in one of her trademark dramatic hats at the wheel of her Stutz-Bearcat (yellow with red cushions), her proud father standing beside her. Bair was in his mid-60's by then, a well-rounded figure in his familiar suit and tie. In one photo, Alberta is dressed in a white suit, ready to lead a parade. Her car is bedecked with flowers and ribbons. Even the steering wheel and spare tire are garlanded in ribbon, as is the hood.

Alberta was always happy to lead the parades.

But problems in the banking industry and the advent of World War I brought an abrupt end to Bair's interest in racing horses and cars.

Chapter 11
THE ROSEBUD LAND AND IMPROVEMENT COMPANY

A Golden Opportunity

In August of 1909, Charlie wrote to Mary from Washington:
"My Dear Mate
Should have writen sooner but had little to write about.
Yegen over bid me on my District but hope to skin him out
yet. soon as I can will hike for home. awful warm here.
Expect to be home some time next week will come on Special
train with Senator Carter and Committee With love to all
as ever yours
C.M. Bair"

Apparently Bair was not able to "skin him out," and he lost
his reservation lease in 1910. After leaving the reservation, he
moved his ranching operations to Martinsdale in Meagher
County. The ranch is situated where the South Fork of the
Musselshell joins the North Fork to form the Musselshell River.
A little over a hundred miles from Billings, it made a longer trip
for Bair to oversee the operation. He maintained his
headquarters at the Northern Hotel in Billings where he kept a
room permanently and also had an office at his lawyers' firm,
Woods and Cooke.

Bair began to expand into other arenas of business. He was
already involved with banking in Billings, and in the course of
the next two decades, Charlie would become involved in oil
exploration, land development, mining, and utilities.

While still running sheep on the reservation and in the
Forsyth area, Bair became involved with the Two Leggins
Irrigation project and the Rosebud Land and Improvement
Company.

After 1900, many farmers were lured to Montana by new
land policies and lots of promotion. Many boosters saw
reclamation as the key to prosperity. The Newlands Reclamation
Act of 1902 committed the federal government to a long-range
program of building large-scale irrigation projects throughout
the arid West.

Peter Larson, Bair's old friend, also had a history of attempting new ventures. He was associated with his brothers-in-law, among others, and was involved in his railroad construction business as well as lumber, mining, banking, real estate promotion, merchandising, and flour mills. (At the time of his death, according to the Helena Independent, he was the largest individual owner of flouring mills west of the Mississippi.) In April, 1904, Articles of Incorporation were filed for the Rosebud Land and Improvement Company and signed by John Edwards of Forsyth, and George Beattie and Peter Larson of Helena. Bair joined them in May.

John Edwards was originally from Illinois, leaving at the age of seventeen to go West. He worked as a cowboy in Colorado and then in northern Texas, coming to Montana in 1889 on a cattle drive. He worked as the superintendent of the Cruse cattle ranch in Fergus county, and then he went into the mercantile business. He was appointed Indian Agent of the Crow Indians, a post he held for three years. Bair began his reservation lease while Edwards was the agent.

Edwards organized the Bank of Commerce in Forsyth and the Richardson Mercantile Company. Bair was associated with the bank, and was listed at one point as the vice-president—a job he did not actively serve in but which was undoubtedly an indication of the monetary interest he held.

Edwards went on to serve in the state Senate and unsuccessfully tried for the national Senate nomination in 1916. He was a part of the "Carter faction" in Montana Republican politics. The one-time cowboy was described as hot-tempered and arrogant but a skilled political manipulator.

The other major participant in the land development company was Edward W. Beattie, although it was his brother George who was originally listed on the articles of incorporation.

George and Edward Beattie came to Montana in 1885 to manage the large estate left by their brother Alexander, and they widely invested in mining, ranching, and real estate, conducting their business as a general partnership. Their most important interests were the Rosebud Land and Improvement Company and the Silver Bow Park addition in Butte. They also had real estate interests in Chouteau County and Great Falls.

Edward Beattie had served as U.S. Surveyor General for Montana from 1897 to 1904; correspondence involving the Rosebud organizer was addressed to General Beattie. He, like Bair and Larson, was an intimate friend of Senator Thomas Carter, who had gotten Beattie the job of Surveyor General.

Charlie Bair, with the help of his lawyer Fred Collins, soon became the major mover and financier for the land company, especially after the death of Thomas Carter in 1911 and General Beattie in 1915.

The cover of a pamphlet distributed by Bair and his partners portrays Uncle Sam turning his back on graveyards and smoldering fires as he enters "Opportunity," passing a road sign "To Montana." Uncle Sam has dropped fliers that read "Oats," "Wheat," "Barley," "Potatoes," "Montana Sugar Beets," and "A Magic Crop in Wonderland." A huge banner ahead reads "Irrigated Lands."

Despite hard work in development and lots of advertising in the East, the project didn't prosper. Money brought in from land sales was put back into ditch repair, a seemingly endless problem.

In 1909, the directors of the company met to consider the advisability of forming an irrigation district in Rosebud County, deciding to call it the "Cartersville Irrigation District."

A newpaper article in 1917 told of Bair's own farming and ranching business near the development project:

"'It costs no more to raise a thoroughbred than it does a scrub,' said Mr. Bair in speaking of his operations recently.

"With this motto in view he has taken a farm of 1,200 acres in the valley of the Big Horn, adjoining the town of Hardin some 60 miles from Billings, and near the Crow Indian Reservation, where he formerly pastured his large flocks, and is making it one of the most [outstanding] pure bred stock farms in the state.

"This farm is irrigated by the Two Leggins canal, built by Mr. Bair and associates to irrigate more than 20,000 acres of fertile land in Big Horn county. He commenced farming it some six years ago. With giant traction engines he turned under the native sod and planted the land to alfalfa with oats as a nurse crop. In the fall of 1910 he probably had the largest field of irrigated oats in the state, nearly 1,200 acres...

"This year he cut the alfalfa crop of 800 acres, harvested sugar beets, some 250 acres and grew grains and cereals on the remainder of the land. This farm he has stocked with the best of animals. His Percheron stallion, the head of the Bair stud, won the grand sweepstakes at the International Livestock show at Chicago. In 1915 he went to the state fair in Helena and bought the grand champion Duroc.

"He bought a Jersey boar, the grand champion Poland China Boar and the red ribbon winner of the Duroc Jerseys as well as some of the champion sows of each breed. This year he went to the Midland Empire fair at Billings and bought the grand champion Poland China boar and four of the prize winning sows of the same breed.

"...He is not raising these animals for show purposes...This year he shipped 700 fatted hogs from the thorough-bred stock to market. He is fattening white faces, a large shipment of which will go the the eastern market this month.

"Having installed the thoroughbred animals in his cattle, horse, and stock pens he turned his attention to the chickens. Hundreds of chickens are raised every year. Recently he instructed the people on his farm to kill off all of the chickens this winter. In the spring he is going to start out with nothing but pure breds and will install Barred Rocks."

The article went on to describe the buildings and machinery including an ice machine for the cold storage. Charlie thought there was a gas field under the ranch and had a well dug. Sure enough, they found gas. Soon the machinery was operated and the buildings were heated by natural gas.

Charlie called the ranch the Alberta Ranch, and would write Alberta telling her how her ranch was doing. This interest for Alberta didn't prevent him from later selling the place, along with the Lower Hardin ranch to the Great Western Sugar Company.

In 1924, the Rosebud Land and Improvement Corporation tried to reorganize and refinance the Cartersville Irrigation District with some limited success, but not until 1934 was the company able to collect a portion of its investment with a "bail-out" from the Reconstruction Finance Corporation.

Fred Collins would sum up the venture in a report to Edmond Silmmons of Denver, one of the stockholders:

"I do not know what has been written you so I don't know how far to go back into past history. It became obvious that this project was doomed to one bad year after another so that farmers no matter how hard they tried could not succeed. The canal got into worse shape all the time, regardless of what the Rosebud Land and Development Co. has spent upon it from the slight income they have had since they spent a lot several years ago trying to put it on a working basis."

Bair still believed in irrigation projects, and later, he had plans drawn up by a Boston firm for $65,000 for a dam and irrigation system on his Martinsdale ranch. He never began that project, but when the state determined to build a dam on the North Fork of the Musselshell, he provided the basis for the Upper Musselshell Water Users Association by giving the state the blueprints he had hired Boston engineers to put together.

The dam and irrigation ditches were installed in the 1930's—on Bair and Court Durand land. The reservoir was named the Durand Reservoir, but in 1968, Governor Tim Babcock and the Water Resources Board renamed it the Bair Reservoir. The governor said it was a small payment for the love and dedication that Charles Bair gave to the state of Montana. He went on to comment that Bair was also "...instrumental, through a large personal contribution, in bringing Montana Power into Martinsdale."

Chapter 12

OILFIELDS AND COALFIELDS

Wyoming and Montana

Charlie Bair watched the coming of the automobile into the country's mainstream and decided oil would become the next gold rush. Then, in 1910, the Great Northern Railroad started to convert some of its coal burning locomotives into oil burners, and Bair added fuel to his interest.

That next year Bair and William Rea went to Mexico to investigate the possibilities of oil exploration. Due to the uncertain Mexican political situation, Charlie was advised to stay away from Mexico, so he turned to possibilites in Montana and Wyoming.

Settlers on a wagon train, crossing the Bighorn River on the Bozeman Trail, were the first to find crude oil in Montana, a pool of water covered with a film of oil which they used to grease their wagon axles. The year was 1864.

Granville Stuart reported the next find of oil in 1880 while looking for a new cattle range in what is now Musselshell and Petroleum counties. He predicted that Montana would one day be an oil producer.

Bair became a pioneer in the oil business in southwestern Montana and northern Wyoming, and he was the first to explore the possibilities of drilling in those areas.

Bair acquired some of his excitement for oil when he became acquainted with E. Howard Hunt in Miles City, who was prospecting for oil but without much success. Bair would often pay Hunt's laundry bill and gave him the use of his room at the Northern when he was in Billings. Hunt later went to Texas where he made his "big find." He never needed anyone to pay for his laundry after that.

Bairoil, Wyoming, in Sweetwater County, forty miles north of Rawlins, became the site of the first well the Bair Oil Company drilled.

The Bair Oil Company was incorporated in Wyoming on August 29, 1916, to "...locate, purchase, lease and otherwise acquire lands, mines, and mineral claims, and particularly lands containing or believed to contain petroleum and other oil springs and deposits; to prospect, drill, mine, bore, and sink wells and shafts; to prepare, produce, refine, pipe, store, transport, supply, buy, sell, manufacture and distribute petroleum and other oils and their products and by-products..."; in other words, to encompass all levels of the oil industry. Its capital stock was listed as $2,500,000, with the 25,000 shares valued at $100 each.

Bair and Fred V.H. Collins put the company into motion with George Brimmer listed as the resident agent at the office in Rawlins.

Drilling operations began in the fall of 1915 around Lost Soldier Butte with a great deal of optimism, tempered somewhat when the company drilled into water in the oil field located on the extreme north end of their property. The company shut down for the winter and began drilling again in the spring as soon as the road conditions permitted. A marker on the new well tells of success: "Lost Soldier—A—Well No. 1. Drilling began June 20 and was completed June 29, 1916. The well delivered 200 barrels a day." A pipeline was soon built to the Union Pacific railroad at Fort Steele.

In the spring the Billings Gazette reported that "...acting through F.V.H. Collins of the firm of Collins, Campbell and Wood, Charles M. Bair of Billings, and F.V.H. Collins of Billings and Forsyth, sold to the Washington-Wyoming Oil Company of Seattle, Washington, a one-half interest in the holdings of the Bair Oil Company of Rawlins. The consideration paid was $250,000 cash."

On Collins' advice, they didn't sell the whole company and retain royalties. However, this was a mistake in light of the quantity of oil taken from the area in later years.

One of the first buildings erected in Bairoil after oil was discovered in 1915 was a boarding house. When it finally closed in 1941, the Republican-Bulletin of Rawlins reported:

"In the boom of the early '20's when most of the work performed was done by hand as many as 300 men ate three meals a day during the peak of the boom along about 1923." The boarding house was the common meeting ground for the oil workers and tradesmen connected with the oil industry, a colorful group that included roustabouts, pumpers, tool dressers, drillers, teamsters, gang pushers, foremen, truck drivers, caretakers, geologists, pipe-liners, machinists, office men and others.

Later, when the main offices of the Prairie Oil and Gas Co. and Sinclair moved to Bairoil, oil company officials and others dined there.

The Bair Oil Company ceased actively operating the boarding house in the early 1930's, but it continued operation under different owners until it closed in 1941.

Good roads, trailer camps adjacent to the oil fields, shorter work days, and other eating places nearby lessened the need for a boarding house in the oil fields.

The Bair Oil Company was dissolved in 1933.

Today, the population of Bairoil, Wyoming is only about 250, sustained by the production work of Amoco. The people of that community mounted a plaque on the first well and remember Bair, the man who drilled it.

Bair was willing to gamble on other ventures as well. In the ranch files are old stock certificates from such companies as Gulf Inland Oil and others that never paid off.

Fred Collins wanted to interest Bair in coal exploration as well as oil, so Charlie backed Collins, who took the lead in the venture.

In 1919, the Billings Gazette reported that the Bair-Collins Coal Company had been incorporated in Billings "with the immediate intention of developing a bituminous coal mine at Painted Robe between Billings and Great Falls on the Great Northern railway..."

Coal in this region was semi-bituminous (hard) and made a cleaner-burning fuel than the softer coal. While the railroads had their own mines, there was also a large market in the home heating area.

The officers of the corporation were Fred V.H. Collins, president; and Charles M. Bair, vice president. The company was capitalized at $500,000.

Fred Collins was a young lawyer who had come from the East to escape the stress of the city. Highly intelligent, he had turned down promising job offers in the East to live in Montana. Collins and Bair formed a deep friendship when Collins served as legal counsel to the Rosebud Land and Livestock Company, and Collins had defended Bair in personal legal issues. Bair was interested in financing Collins' incursion into the coal industry.

Lewis and Clark first mentioned the presence of coal seams along the Missouri River in 1805 when they passed through Montana on their momentous journey. Manuel Lisa, a Spanish fur trader, used coal to heat his buildings at the mouth of the Big Horn River on the banks of the Yellowstone in 1807.

Coal mines near Bannack, Argenta, and Virginia City supplied coal for the gold camps in the 1860's. When the Northern Pacific came through in 1883, it bought a mine out of Helena and developed it. The vein was exhausted by 1906 and the railroad moved to Carbon County and opened a mine at Red Lodge.

The Milwaukee and St. Paul Railroad went through Musselshell County, and it was here that Collins wanted to develop his mine. The new mine at Painted Robe was called the Silver Tip Mine and the coal was marketed as Silver Tip Coal. Plans were also made to develop an area in the Carpenter Creek field which was adjacent to the Milwaukee Railroad.

In 1921, following a serious strike in the coal industry in Roundup, the company bought the Keene Mine at Roundup.

Bair left the running of the company to Collins. Collins told Bair that people often thought his name was Bair Collins, and even, he added jokingly, referred to him as "Bare Collins."

The Hardin Light and Power Company and the Forsyth Light and Power Company were also listed on the company stationery. John Edwards of Forsyth was also involved in the organization, but did not appear on the letterhead.

A letter from Collins to Bair in 1925 mentions a "blow-up" between Bair and Edwards, precipitating the sale of the power and light companies. Collins' explanation of his payment to Edwards of $25,000 is interesting to follow as he juggles payments and credits to his partners.

"When you and Edwards blew up you had $6250 invested in Hardin and Forsyth plants—I paid Edwards $25,000 for his 1/2 interest in cash altho I have before me an apprasial of both plants by the Montana Power Co. offering $50,000 cash for them, and they owed you at that time $31,000 borrowed money and owed the Bank of Commerce $15,000 and the debts were a total of $46,000 or almost as much as Montana Power offered - but if you and John blew up any further there might have been lots of results so I paid him $25,000 for his interest and then started to see if your investment could not be saved and my own also. I got $25,000 Bair Collins Co. stock for the Edwards interest and you got $25,000 stock for your interest altho your stock only cost $6250. Then you also got $31,000 stock for what the plants owed you...

"You have put up in cash at different times for Bair Collins Co. stock $50,500.

"...I only hope that in 1926 I can pay dividends to you amounting at least to $22,649.38 and when that is done you will have every dollar back you have invested and your interest in the Bair Collins Co. and its property and anything that comes after it thereafter will be velvet..."

At the end of 1928, Bair's cash investment was down to $10,880.63, so presumably the dividends through the 1930's paid off that investment, although there was not a great deal of profit in the coal venture for Bair.

During the 1920's and 1930's, Bair stopped in Roundup on his way to look at cattle he had out in the Musselshell Valley and always called at the office. Yearly, he presented his partner Collins with a white Cadillac. Bair's family had a new white Cadillac every year, as well, a tradition that continued after his death.

Lillian Gildroy Kirkpatrick, who worked for the Bair-Collins Company from 1921 to 1954, would recall Bair's visits to the Roundup office with great nostalgia. She considered him a straight-forward businessman with great acumen, but at the same time a very human, caring person.

During the Depression of the 1930's, Bair helped many of his neighboring ranchers by giving them free coal.

When the company's Star Mine at Musselshell was closed in 1936, the Bair-Collins Company donated 25 buildings to the Billings Polytechnic Institute which is now Rocky Mountain College.

The Billings Gazette reported that the buildings which formerly housed the miners would enable the school to provide ten faculty residences, a mill and seedhouse, a large barn, a hospital unit, and other improvements, both at the Billings campus and at their summer camp on the Stillwater River.

Collins, who had formed another company, the F.V.H.

Collins Company, also headquartered at Roundup, died in 1941 in Arizona and was buried at Forsyth where he had owned the Porcupine Ranch.

Bair kept his interest in the coal company. After his death, the Bair Company retained interest until 1954. With diesels replacing old steam engines on the railroad and the conversion of household heating to gas or electricity, the coal business was no longer viable.

The company was in debt, but rather than declare bankruptcy as the lawyers advised, Alberta and Marguerite spent $250,000 to pay off the creditors and dissolve the company in 1954. The daughters felt their father would have wanted it that way.

Chapter 13
ART
The "Biltmore Gang" and the Sharp Connection

Not all the men who came to Montana were businessmen and glory seekers. Some came to portray the West. George Catlin was dubbed "Montana's first press agent." He came to Montana on the first steamboat in 1832.

Catlin had been born in Wyoming but was taken at an early age to Philadelphia where he grew up to become a lawyer. After seeing a party of Western Indians who were visiting Philadelphia, he left the practice of law and went West to record the history and customs of Native Americans in his paintings. Karl Bodmer came in 1833 with Prince Maximilian of Prussia to record the Prince's visit to America. John James Aububon spent the summer of 1843 painting the birds and animals around Fort Union. Frederic Remington, Charles Russell, Ralph De Camp, E.S. Paxson, O.C. Seltzer, and Joseph Henry Sharp were other wonderful artists who recorded the Old West.

Charlie Bair first met Charles Russell in Helena before the turn of the century and bought a watercolor from him. He met Joseph Sharp when he leased land on the Crow Reservation.

Henry, as Sharp was known to his friends, and wife Addie had come to Crow Agency in the summer of 1899. Sharp was drawn by the culture of the Crows, the proximity to Custer battlefield, and a great desire to paint the Plains Indians before their culture became changed by the white man. Sharp had previous experience with the Indians of the Southwest, where he was a charter member of the Taos Society of Artists.

Phoebe Hearst, widow of Senator George Hearst and mother of William Randolph Hearst, bought seventy-nine paintings from Sharp in the spring of 1901 for $6,500. This tremendous sale allowed Sharp to resign his teaching position and to devote himself full-time to the work of portraying the Indians.

Mrs. Hearst bought another $1,000 worth of Sharp's paintings later in 1901, and she further contracted to buy fifteen more paintings each year thereafter for five years. Sharp's paintings were hung in a memorial building for Senator Hearst at the University of California at Berkeley, donated by Mrs. Hearst on behalf of the Chair of Indian Research.

On previous visits to Crow Agency, the Sharps had stayed in the Server Hotel. They stayed there in the summer of 1902, but only long enough to build a permanent home, where they lived summers and winters, spending springs in Taos, New Mexico. They also spent some time in California where Addie had relatives.

The Guil Reynolds family had just come to the reservation where Reynolds was to serve as agent. Carolyn Reynolds Reibeth, the Reynolds' second child, recalled that the studio was built first, so that Sharp could get to his work.

The Sharp house was built of log, one of only three at the agency. The woods at the agency were mostly cottonwoods, box elders, and ash, so the pine for logs had to be brought some distance.

Many worked on the house, said Mrs. Reibeth, including Henry and Addie. Reynolds supplied the agency carpenter, and one account mentions "prison labor," the men from the guard house on the reservation. They worked under the charge of "Smokey," the "black man of all labors" around the agency. Smokey's real name was Charles Wilson. He'd been born a slave, but he'd come to Montana as a young boy. Later he broke horses for the cavalry, and at the agency, he tended the cows and horses and acted as a policeman, mail carrier, and whatever else was required.

The interior of the Sharp home reflected the travels of the Sharps with an abundance of Indian artifacts and rugs, Roycrofter and Mission furniture, Japanese print curtains, and blue and white Willow Ware English china. Sharp later enlarged his studio, and also erected a buffalo hide tepee which he sometimes used as a studio. Many of his fine "tepee" pictures were painted there.

Another studio was a sheep wagon, a gift of Charlie Bair. Bair and Sharp installed a mica skylight in the sheep wagon which allowed better light. This was a boon to Sharp, for it allowed him to go to all parts of the reservation to paint out of doors in the winter. He removed all the "furniture" of the wagon, except for the stove. Often, he'd paint at night in the winter until his paint froze, then crawl into the wagon, thaw his paints, and paint some more.

J.H. Sharp and "Prairie Dog," his sheepwagon studio, circa 1900. Courtesy Buffalo Bill Historical Center, Cody, Wyoming.

Bair gave orders to his camp tenders to stock the studio wagon when they went to the reservation to supply the sheepherder wagons. Sharp called his wagon "The Prairie Dog."

Bair also fitted the artist with a Stetson. Sharp wrote to Marguerite Bair Lamb years later: "...My, the memories your letter calls up! The many, many fine studies made from the sheep wagon studio when it was below zero—the visits to Billings and the eats! Tell Dad I have the Stetson he gave me—it is rather disreputable but I can't give it up."

The Sharps visited the Bairs often in their Billings home, and the families became warm friends. Addie played the piano for them. Marguerite and her parents eagerly sought Addie's advice about Marguerite's musical education. When Marguerite went East to study music, she went to Addie's old school, the Cincinnati Conservatory of Music.

Bair gave Sharp a stack of photographs from his days in the Klondike—pictures of native huts, art, dog teams, and prospectors.

Charlie became one of Sharp's best customers. One Christmas, Bair sent the Sharps a large box of apples. The artist borrowed an old wooden bowl from Carrie Reynolds and painted a still life with the apples in the bowl and a vase with sprigs of holly. Another work he painted showed the box, still with the address on it and still full of apples, with a few scattered around.

Bair bought both paintings, had them framed, and gave the one with the box to the Reynolds. The other he kept, and today it hangs in the dining room of the Bair home. Later, Alberta thought the Reynolds would have liked the one with the Reynolds heirloom bowl, but no exchange was made.

Bair gave another painting entitled "The Little Chief" to the Billings Chamber of Commerce in 1915 (subsequently donated to the Yellowstone County Fine Arts Center in 1967).

Senator Joseph Dixon also received a gift of a Sharp—"a quiet October afternoon on the Little Horn River, Crow Reservation." Bair was appreciative of the help Dixon had given him in the Congressional hearings following the charges made by Helen Grey in 1907.

Other paintings still in the Bair home today include scenes from the reservation, a small Indian portrait, and a large scene of "Charles' favorite fishing hole" on the Little Big Horn. Another small oil of an encampment was done for Alberta. On the back is the inscription, "To Alberta—a real hickory chip of the old smoked block From J.H. Sharp 1906." Alberta was about eleven when the painting was done for her.

Sharp also gave the Bairs some Indian artifacts from his collection. One artifact, a pair of beaded leggings, still has a card in the pocket in Sharp's handwriting: "Rain in the Face pant North Hump Crow who threatened to clip heart of General Custer 1904." Sharp had a deep interest in the Custer Battle and the Indians from that period on, and he painted any he could locate.

By 1908 models were harder to get on the reservation, and Addie had begun to develop emotional problems. They took off for a summer vacation and returned to the agency during the winter of 1909-1910. Matters did not improve. Sharp was in failing health as well, and so, in the spring, they went to see medical specialists and then moved back to Taos.

Since Bair had moved his family to Portland that year, the friendship between the families was reduced to occasional correspondence. The Bairs were in Portland when Sharp made his infrequent trips to Billings to bring exhibits to the Parmly Billings Memorial Library. His last visit to Billings was in 1923, but he exhibited only for the Reynolds in their home.

After Marguerite's marriage to Dave Lamb, Marguerite wrote to Sharp to tell him the news, and to ask if he would do her own portrait. Sharp responded, "Now about your portrait—that used to be my biz, and was trained a portrait and figure painter, but I haven't painted a white person since 'Sissy' [Carolyn Reynolds] at Crow Agency many years ago. I would be afraid to try..."

Declining an invitation to visit, he wrote, "...nothing in the world would I like better, and to meet Mr. Lamb. I'm really glad at all you say. You have missed a lot out of life, but making it up now. The trouble with me is that practically all my work and biz is done in and from Taos during the six-seven months of summer. through roads and many travelers, with Taos a stong drawing card. If we leave there for even a week or two it knocks things all awry, so we do our traveling in winter-mostly Honolulu and Orient, Mex. So.Am. etc.

"I've always said I would paint in Taos until I was 80- then get a high powered car and some girls and go out and have some fun. We have the high powered car in Taos, and I was 80 last Sept. but the girls! want to go along? And how about 'Alfalfa' [Alberta]..."

The Bairs and Sharps stayed in contact after the reservation days. When the Bairs moved back to Montana from Portland, they asked Sharp to buy some European paintings for them on one of his trips East. He bought three or four typical, somber European paintings. The Bairs planned to use European paintings with their European furniture. Later, however, they incorporated the Russells, Sharps, and the works of other western artists with their furniture, and the blend worked well.

In California the Bairs' friendship with Charlie Russell and his wife Nancy flourished. The Russells began going to

California for the winters in 1919. By then, Russell's reputation was established, and Nancy found California a good place to market her husband's work.

The Bairs stayed at the Biltmore in Los Angeles, and Russell exhibited in the gallery there. As soon as the Bairs arrived at the hotel, there would be a message from Russell: "Come see me. Charlie."

Bair and Russell, along with Will Rogers, the cowboy columnist, humorist, and actor, and movie cowboys William S. Hart, Charlie Mack, and Tom Mix got together almost daily at the gallery to tell stories and recall the old days of the West. Hart was the model of the strong, silent hero of the West; Mix was a U.S. Marshall who had turned actor and starred in more than 400 low-budget westerns; and Mack was a cowboy-turned-actor. They all liked to visit about the "Wild West" that was no more.

Edward M. Curtis, a well-known photographer of Indians, had a studio in the Biltmore as well. Curtis had been a friend of the Bairs from reservation days. Bair had bought several of the Curtis Indian folios when the photographer needed money. Curtis had also been a member of the party the day Bair took the Jesserands to visit the Crows.

Edward Curtis photograph of artist Charles M. Russell, Los Angeles, 1925.

Edward Curtis photograph of Charlie Bair, Los Angeles, 1925.

Marguerite and Alberta had long wanted a good picture of their father, but he refused to sit for his portrait. The girls told Curtis their problem and he told them,"You get your Dad and Charlie Russell to come down to my studio for a visit, and I'll get their pictures without them knowing." Curtis was able to get good portraits of the two which today sit side by side on a mantle in the Bair home.

The Bairs enjoyed the Southern California climate. Bair at one time thought they should buy a yacht and go "bob-sledding over the waves," but after one afternoon fishing on the ocean, Bair was deathly ill, and the idea of the yacht was tabled. They took in the sights and attended the polo matches at Coronado. And there were dinners among the families.

Charlie, Mary, and Alberta at a polo match in California.

When Bill Hart entertained, the group went to his Horseshoe Ranch at Newhall, California. Alberta recalled a long winding road, often muddy and slick in the California rains, leading to the top of a hill where the ranch house sat. Once, as they crept up the muddy incline with Alberta at the wheel, Bair leaned over and said, "Toddy, do you ever think to check the water in the battery?"

Alberta was taken aback, but later realized it was her father's way of taking her mind off the condition of the road.

The Russells usually entertained at their home as well. On one occasion, Russell had just done a sculpture of three bears. Bair asked Alberta, "Toddy, should we buy that set of bears?"

"Oh," Alberta replied, "if only there were four instead of three!"

Alberta recalled that they could have had anything they wanted from Russell, but they never thought much about it. They just enjoyed the friendship.

Bair did buy some things from Russell and told the girls to "hang onto them" since they might be worth a great deal of money someday. When the Bair family returned to Montana from Portland, the Russell pictures were stored in the root cellar for some time. When Nancy Russell wrote to ask to include the pictures in a book she was compiling of her late husband's work, she was told the pictures were unavailable since they were stored in the root cellar. The Bairs didn't hear from her again. However, the increasing interest in Russell art eventually brought them out to share the walls with the Sharps.

One story Alberta recalls from that time paints a revealing portrait of the Russells themselves:

One evening while Marguerite and Alberta Bair were having dinner at the Ambassador Hotel, the Russells came in with guests and were seated behind the girls. Russell tapped Alberta on the shoulder and started a long visit until Nancy intervened. She called Alberta to their table and introduced the guests who appeared bored, stiff, wealthy—certainly, potential buyers of art. They were dressed in formal wear for dinner. Russell was in his usual dress-up clothes: tuxedo, red sash, and cowboy boots. The artist was as bored as his guests, leaving Nancy to do business and entertain. When Russell got a chance, he leaned over to Alberta and inquired, "Has Charlie heard from Pink-Eye lately?"

"Oh, yes," and Alberta was off on her tale.

Pink-Eye O'Conner, a sheepherder, had just killed a man and had written her father that the killing was entirely justified and that if Bair would send him the money for a lawyer, he would work for Bair for nothing for the rest of his life. (Pink-Eye was 65 at the time.) Bair made a special trip to Montana to appear as a character witness and to help his old herder.

It was an interesting case. The sheepherder was accused of killing a popular cowboy named Pat Loney. The state based its prosecution on the fact that the herder was bitter toward Loney because Loney had often baited him by riding through his sheep bands on the Philbrook Rosebud Range. On the last occasion, the State contended that Pink-Eye had opened up the sheep wagon door and shot Loney as he stood at the wagon neck yoke where he had dismounted from his horse. He died instantly, and O'Conner left him there for four days while cooking and sleeping in his wagon.

Bair, I.D. O'Donnell of Billings, and other former employers of O'Conner testified that there was "...not a vicious drop of blood in his body and that he never awakened in the morning with a speck of malice in his heart toward anybody."

O'Conner testified that Loney shot himself accidentally and that further the creeks were swollen and that he was seven miles from the Newell Philbrick headquarters on the Rosebud; that he couldn't leave the "sheps" unless he could take the "sheps" with him as that was his training; and for that reason, he stayed with the body for four days. Under vigorous cross-examination, he kept repeating, "I couldn't leave the sheps" and "Him was dead anyway."

Bair testified that when Pink-Eye was in his employ, his band was caught in a blizzard, and they found most of the band dead in a cut-bank area; but O'Conner was still with them, half frozen and half-starved.

A hog was shaved and shot and introduced to the jury, showing body burns, and even the face skin of the victim was produced to show that he had been shot in the face, but O'Conner was finally acquitted. Pink-Eye's friends "put up a very generous purse" and saw him and his little dog off on a train for Colorado.

Russell and Alberta spent the evening having a good time talking about Pink-Eye while Nancy and the prospective purchasers sat in silence. This was about the time that Russell sold a painting to Douglas Fairbanks for $10,000 and another to the Prince of Wales for $10,000.

In 1926, following Russell's death, the Bairs received a Christmas card from Nancy Russell with the note, "Charlie made this sketch for our Christmas card this year and I wish to add my appreciation for the flowers and your sympathetic message to Jack and me." Other memories from the Russell friendship include a personalized envelope and the Curtis photograph of Russell that stands by that of Bair on the mantle in the Pine Room.

"Waiting for a Chinook," the "report" on the terrible winter of 1886-1887, originally titled "The Last of the Five Thousand," was sent by Jesse Phelps to his ranching partner, Louis Kaufman. It was then in the possession of Wallis Huidekoper who ranched out of Two Dot. Nancy asked Bair repeatedly to help her get the picture back, but Bair was reluctant to pressure his neighbor, and the picture remained with Huidekoper. Huidekoper later gave the picture to the Montana Stockgrowers Association, and it now hangs in the Russell Gallery of the Montana Historical Society in Helena.

Following the death of Rogers, Hart wrote to Bair, "It is so good to hear from you. It really cheers me up a lot. I get mighty blue at times. I knew dear old Charlie Russell since 1901—Bill Rogers since 1905—Charlie Mack since 1910. And they're all gone. Two cut down by tragic accidents and one before his time. I seem to hang on. I'm in great shape...."

In the same letter, Hart commented on the statue of himself which now stands above the Rimrocks in Billings. The statue had been originally planned for North Dakota, but Bair got it for Billings.

The unveiling of the Bill Hart Monument took place during a Founder's Day Celebration, July 2-4 in 1927. Photos taken by Peter Billings of the event are revealing. The real-life Hart faces the life-sized bronze of the movie cowboy and his horse. Of the two, the bronze is the more dominant, the more heroic-looking. The cheekbones are more pronounced; the chin is more determined; the stance is more assured. The real-life Hart sports the beginnings of a pot belly. To the right of the bronze stands Bair, the man responsible for bringing the statue to Billings. By then, Bair is 62, and his figure is portly. With his hands he seems to orchestrate the details of the unveiling with an air of concern.

The Hart statue was done by Charles Christadoro. At the dedication ceremonies, Hart called the West, "The land of

From left: Guil Reynolds, Bill Hart, Charlie Bair at the unveiling of the Hart statue on the Billings Rims.

staunch comradeship, of kindly sympathy, of kindred intellect, where hearts beat high and hands grip firm, where poverty is no disgrace and where charity never grows cold..."

Now he wrote "...I love what you say of the old Pinto and the bronze cowpuncher high up on the rimrock. It is good to know that they will always keep guard over the Valley of the Yellowstone. It gives me a warm glow to think of them."

Dick Logan, the airport manager at that time, said that Bair, "Martinsdale sheep rancher and intimate of Hart," had donated the money to add a brand to the statue horse. Bair stipulated that the horse bear the brand of an outfit headed by Russell when he was "farmhanding" in the Great Falls country. Hart agreed with the choice. Bair realized the long-continuing importance of brands in Montana since he had begun concentrating on the ranch at Martinsdale.

Another well-known Western artist and writer, Will James, was a friend of the Bair family although he was never a part of the "Biltmore gang," partly because Hart thought James was a "fake." James had worked for Hart as a stunt man in the movies. Although Hart was trained as a Shakespearean actor, when he became a cowboy actor he required that the portrayal be authentic. He never thought James was a very good cowboy.

The Bairs' friendship with James flourished during the 1940's, when James made his home in Billings and lived there until his death. Charlie Bair and his family had room for all in their circle of friends.

Chapter 14
A NEW HOME BASE
The Martinsdale Ranch

When Bair lost his grazing lease in 1910 on the Crow Reservation, he concentrated his ranching activities in the Musselshell Valley. Along with the Martinsdale ranch, he leased extensive range, and as land became available, he would buy it and add to the Bair ranch. Because of the Great Depression and the many years of drought, many small homesteaders gave up their land in the 1920's and 1930's and were happy to have someone who could pay them, instead of losing their land for back taxes.

The Musselshell Valley in central Montana was settled early by sheep and cattle ranchers. The old Carroll Trail wound through the area on the way to Canyon Ferry and Helena. It was a rich and wide-open country and good winter range for cattle.

Ed Sayre, a pioneer stockman of the area, reported to the local newspaper in December of 1875 that the Musselshell had about 10,000 head of cattle and more were coming in for winter grazing. Before many years, it was necessary for the stockmen to band together for spring and fall roundups—in the spring for branding and in the fall for shipping.

The Musselshell Association rounded up cattle in the entire valley, a distance of over 150 miles and from 40 to 70 miles across. In 1878, the first large roundup in the Musselshell used sixty men and about 300 head of horses. The cattlemen followed a pattern of fanning out in all directions from one area, to gather cattle and move them to a designated location and corrals. They repeated the same process each day until the entire range was covered.

The tough winter of 1886-1887 put an end to the great roundups and the open range. One rancher lost 1,500 sheep in one storm, another lost 700 in the blizzard, and yet another lost 500 in one snow slide. Cattle losses ran 20 to 25 percent.

Martinsdale, the town located at the confluence of the South Fork of the Musselshell and the North Fork of the Musselshell, survived along with many of the old ranches.

The Gauglers first settled Martinsdale in 1876 and built a general outfitting store named Gauglersville, and within a month they added a hotel. The little settlement served the few ranchers who had settled in the Musselshell Valley and the travelers who used the Carroll Road which linked Fort Benton with Helena.

Richard Clendennin moved his family to the Forks of the Musselshell in 1877, near the North Fork and directly across from Gauglersville on the South Fork; there he established a store and hotel.

The Bair Company's original cattle brand came with the Martinsdale Ranch. It is a figure "7" under a capital "A" commemorating the date, August 7, 1877, when Richard Clendennin established the Clendennin Ranch. Clendennin made a bid for a postal route, and in 1879 a mail route was inaugurated between White Sulphur Springs and Martinsdale which soon extended to Lewistown. Another route went from Martinsdale to Coulson (Billings).

By 1885, there was a lively town at "Old Martinsdale" with hotel, livery stable, pool hall, saloons, and store, all of which Clendennin rented to the settlers, except for the hotel, which the family ran. In 1884, Gaugler admitted defeat and sold his stock

Martinsdale scene about 1908. Courtesy of Victor Conway.

of pails, harnesses, red flannel, and tobacco. The property was sold to Reinholdt Kleinschmidt, then to P.H. Clark, and finally to the Settle family. John Potter, William Lupold, and William Gordon took over the Clendennin ranch in 1894, with Potter as resident manager.

The Montana Railroad was built through the valley in 1899, an extension of the line originally planned to run from Helena to Castle to ship out silver ore. The line was dubbed the "Jawbone" because it was said the builder, John Harlow, had built most of the line on "jawbone" rather than ready cash. The line was finished to Castle in 1896, only to have its usefulness gone after the silver panic destroyed the silver mining industry. In order to salvage the project, Harlow proceeded to build farther down the Musselshell Valley. The Montana Railroad (later the Milwaukee Railroad) reached the forks in 1899. The tracks ran two miles south of Martinsdale, so the town packed up and moved to the tracks making a "new" Martinsdale. "Old" Martinsdale remained the ranch headquarters for the Martinsdale Land and Livestock Ranch.

During these years, the ranch wasn't very profitable and continued to change ownership. In 1905, the ranch was reorganized as the Martinsdale Land and Livestock Company

Martinsdale ranch hands. Courtesy of Victor Conway.

with James Vestal, C.M. Bair, William Rea, and George Corwin as owners. Vestal was the manager.

One of the men Vestal hired was "Goldie" Cornelius Conway, a young Irishman from Missouri. Vestal made him foreman when Conway was only 24, and he stayed until Vestal died a few years later; Conway then succeeded him as manager. Bair was the only stockholder who objected to the new manager, because he wanted a more experienced man who could speculate by buying and selling stock to the advantage of the company. It wasn't Bair's nature to allow the ranch to lose money or even to break even.

Conway was "itching to go it alone" and took his dismissal with good grace. He liked and respected Bair, but he did comment that Bair lived by the Golden Rule: "He who has the gold makes the rules."

William Rae was a charming, handsome fellow who never called at the Bair home without chocolates for the ladies, but although a gentleman, he was apparently a poor player in the business world. He seemed to lose money on whatever enterprise he ventured into. He'd been in partnership with Bair with sheep in the Billings and Forsyth areas, and it had been Rae who had interested Bair in the Martinsdale ranch. Rae needed money again for some other financial ventures, so in 1915, Bair bought out Rea and Corwin and the corporation was again reorganized with Bair as principal owner. Gerald Corwin remained as the manager until 1921.

Charlie chasing sheep.

Bair pursued many other ventures but still found time to check on the ranch. As with his sheep business on the reservation, the frequent trips to oversee the operation made his business more profitable. An old saying on the range was that the owner's shadow made the best fertilizer.

In 1934, Mary Bair became very ill. Marguerite and Mary had traveled from Billings to Portland, leaving Alberta in Billings with her father, who had slipped between two cars loading sheep and broken his collarbone.

When Marguerite called Billings to report that the doctors had diagnosed Mary with cancer and had recommended surgery, Alberta immediately left for Portland. On the train, she read an article about amoebic dysentery that had been spread from Chicago. Since Mary had been in Chicago at the Palmer House in the summer to attend the Century of Progress Exposition, Alberta wondered if this wasn't her mother's problem.

In the meantime, Bair had visited with some St. Paul bankers at the Billings bank, and when he reported his wife's illness, they urged him to take her to the Mayo Clinic. Alberta and Marguerite took their mother on the train to St. Paul, with Charlie joining the train in Billings. The bankers had arranged for the Bairs' arrival at the clinic.

Portrait of Mary Bair, taken in Portland.

Doctors soon relieved the family's fears: Mary did not have cancer after all; she had amoebic dysentery! Surgery might have killed her.

The near-tragedy prompted the family to take another look at their far-flung life style. Mary asked Bair where he would like to live permanently, and when he said, "Montana," the decision was made to move back—not to Billings but to the ranch on the Musselshell.

At the start of Prohibition, Bair and two other Billings gentlemen bought the entire liquor stock at the Northern Hotel. Bair had his share moved to Martinsdale. Over the years the labels had vanished, so guests at the Bair home were treated to some surprises until the supply was gone.

As Bair made his permanent home at Martinsdale, the ranch consisted of 60,000 deeded acres with about that much more leased land. He continued to run sheep along with cattle, and in 1931, he was running about 23,000 head of sheep.

Bair leased the Fergus Ranch near Lewistown for some of the sheep, leased land around Ingomar, and even tried leasing around Glacier Park on the Indian Reservation. Bair sent railroad cars of feed for the sheep; unfortunately, an

Charlie in yearling sheep pens.

underhanded agent sold the feed to the Indians and pocketed the cash. That and losses from the bands to "mutton rustlers" prompted Bair to cancel his lease and keep his sheep closer to home where he could keep an eye on them.

Charlie leased land at Wilsall thirty miles south of Martinsdale and bought supplies at the Wilsall store rather than shipping them in from Billings. The owners of the store would years later tell Alberta that Charlie Bair kept them from going under during the Depression.

Bair stopped at one farm and bought garden produce and eggs as he went about his inspection tours. Alberta wondered why he bought eggs when they had a flock of chickens at Martinsdale. Bair explained, "Toddy, those people are barely making it. I wanted to help them."

As Bair went on his rounds to check his sheep, he also checked on some of his old retired herders. Planning to visit "Bill" one day, and knowing his love of liquor and his lack of money, Bair stuck a bottle in the car. After visiting for a few minutes, Bair pulled the bottle out, and offering it to Bill said, "How about a drink, Bill?"

Bill didn't know when his next chance might be so he upended the bottle and drank about a third before he finally stopped for breath and handed the bottle back to Charlie.

"No, no, you keep it, Bill."

"Gawd damn it, Charlie," Bill said. "Why didn't you say that at first? You nearly killed me."

The Depression caused Bair to cut his number of sheep, but he had enough reserves to keep afloat at a time when many others were going under. He was also able to keep going because he knew how to make the best of any situation. For instance, Bair refused to sell his lambs in 1931 at the prices offered and put them in a feedlot in Iowa, shipping them to Chicago later for sale. He personally went back and sorted and shipped the sheep after they'd been on feed, and in his usual fashion of seeing that all was well, he'd change the bands to another farmer if he thought the feed was short. He also kept his wool clip that year because of low prices, a luxury most sheepmen couldn't afford.

In January of 1932, Charlie was back in Des Moines to deliver another shipment of fattened lambs to the Chicago market. He kept his family informed of his travels with his frequent letters addressed to "Dearest Mate, Marguerite and Alberta, ...we will have 6 car loads on the Monday market it has been hard to get them fat in this rain and mud and have been trying to stall them off from shipping until the poultry got cleaned out of the markets thinking the lamb market would advance but only God knows what it will do I brought Mr. Rae along down here. He is a dandy in helping to sort the fat lambs and we got stuck in the ditch the other day in the snow and mud and two trucks couldn't pull us out. Had to get farmer with his tractor...will have to change 2 more bunches of lambs to get them in better hands in order to get them fat as some of these farmers never fed anything but hogs and do not know much at that...."

Another day or so later: "...If the market does not break will do much better with the lambs than what we were offered for them in Montana will have 6 car loads on the Chicago market tomorrow...Had a hard day yesterday loaded lambs in the storm until 8 p.m. they had to bring them so far in the snow had to get the county snow to plow out the road to get them thru at all. I wired Chicago to take care of them this evening on arrival and feed and water them good as they had a hard siege in getting on the cars. I changed 3 car loads and got them a better home where they will be taken care of and get fat. This is a great life if you don't weaken. We drove 40 miles on our way home last night for dinner and had a most delicious dinner and then drove 40 miles home...Mr. Rea came along down with me. He is a peach to help sort and count. His appetite is good he said he did not want any pay just expences [sic] so we are getting along fine."

Two days later, he reported, "...we sure topped the market last week and they say the little fellows walked down the alley in the yards like exporters...."

In February, Bair was checking the sheep in Montana. From Lewistown, where the sheep were on the Fergus ranch, he went to the Rindal ranch where he had sheep on shares, to Spring Creek to see the bunches there, to Forest Grove, and to Geyser.

"Then comes the hard task as the 2500 we have over at Geyser I am compelled to hunt a new home for which is quite difficult this time of the year but will find a place for them somewhere but am afraid will be

Wool growers convention, Butte.

delayed here several days yet on that account. They are good sheep and they must be taken care of....No news but take good care of yourselves and Muzzie and have a good time and I will be with you just as soon as possible."

When someone asked him to contribute to the Red Cross, Charlie remarked that everything had been going out and nothing coming in for him, but he would gladly deliver a carload of sheep to Billings for use in the Red Cross work.

The Martinsdale ranch was one of the largest in the area. Dick Indreland, a Norwegian immigrant, who broke horses for the Bair Company in the late 1920's and 1930's, recalled twenty-five or thirty teams going into the fields for haying. In addition, eight or nine pack trains (with five to a train) were used for camp tending for the sheep bands. Some of the sheep range was at the far end of Meagher County in the Tenderfoot, a trail of seventy or eighty miles from the home ranch. Bair built a cabin in the valley to serve as a commissary for his sheepherders. As it became more difficult to trail sheep with more traffic and more fences, Bair finally stopped using the Tenderfoot and leased it to neighbors on Shannon Creek.

One of Bair's fellow sheepmen out of Harlowton continued to trail his sheep to range in the Belt Mountains. He took a month to get to the mountains, grazed there a month, and took a month to get back to his home ranch. Many days of those two months of travel were on Bair land, just out of sight of the ranch activity. Bair chewed his cigar but remained friends with the man. Bair knew the sheep game.

Charlie was usually able to spot good men. He hired Jim Bowman, originally from Texas, as his foreman because he had a feel for the land and the animals. Bowman asked Indreland if he could hitch up six horses strung out—he wanted to put in a ditch. Indreland asked him if he was going to use a tripod or use a board to survey the ditch. Bowman said, "Follow me." He got on a saddle horse, and led the way as Indreland and the six horses with a ditcher followed. The ditch not only ran water but was being used fifty years later.

It took about a hundred men on the payroll to use the hundreds of horses and work the ranch during that period. The neighboring Smith Brothers ranch was about the same size as the Bair ranch, and between the two, they kept the town of

Martinsdale going.

Bair's involvement was strictly a hands-on experience. Family photographs show him branding cattle in his three-piece suit, hat, and tie, although in one photograph he has conceded to the cold Montana spring weather by wearing a heavy ribbed sweater over his suit. Other photos show him shearing sheep in warmer weather—he wears his vest, hat, and tie, but he has discarded the jacket. Another photo shows an older, stern-looking Bair, possibly in his late sixties or early seventies, wearing eye-glasses, staring down a sheepdog that may have been sleeping on the job.

Fishing wasn't an invitation to informal wear, either. One photo shows Bair digging for worms with an L.A. business associate. Although Bair has taken off his coat, he wore a white shirt and hat, his pants held up by suspenders and arcing gently over his pot belly. Another later photograph shows Bair ice fishing. He leans on one elbow, a glass jar for bait nearby. He is wearing a heavy suit jacket over his suit with snow boots on his feet. With his fedora hat worn bowler-style on his head, he cuts a jaunty figure. Possibly, Bair's characteristic clothing provides clues to his personality: his steadfastness of purpose, his attention to detail. His suits were hand-tailored in Chicago of the finest material. However, this ambition seems tempered by his informal manner—a willingness to have a good time, no matter what the circumstances.

Bair never retired. He always went to town himself to hire men or handle ranch business. He had sheep and cattle in other parts of the state, and he would frequently check on them, too. He never learned to drive, but he kept a driver busy and, in fact, changed drivers often as he wore them out. Finding himself without a driver one day, he went to where Indreland was working horses.

"Dick, I know you can drive those horses, but can you drive a car?"

"Vell," replied Indreland, "I can drive a regular car, but I don't know about dat big one of yours." Bair had a LaSalle at the time.

"They should all work the same—come on, I've got to check some sheep at Ingomar." Bair put Indreland into the driver's seat and crawled into the back to nap on the way down. He woke up just out of Forsyth and asked where they were.

"My gawd, man, are you going to take all day to get there?" Even at the age of 83, he and his chauffeur drove over 33,000 miles in a year.

During the fall of 1932, when Bair was 75, he wrote from Lewistown, "...I am sort of on my toes over here with more sheep on the trail than anybody. Just got in and called Frank Madison but they say he is not at home so I am starting down to the bad lands with John Hill will be back day after tomorrow. I am delighted with the weather and am feeling fine have been sleeping out quite a little up in the mountains among the whispering pines and believe it is good for a fellow. I am getting things straightened out for winter I think in good shape have all the sheep all sorted and on their way 2 bands for Forsyth 5000 and one band on the trail for the bad lands and 4000 for the Fergus Ranch and am trying to arrange to winter the lambs here down in this country instead of trailing them so far up home as the feed is much better in this country. Hoping this finds you all well and happy Lots of love from Dad."

A few days later he wrote from Winnett, "Well I am on my way to the Bad Lands after 2 of the toughest days ever. the Federal Land Bank turned the Fergus Ranch I had leased back to the people who formerly owned it and left me out in the cold with 4000 sheep on my hands and no place to go and not enough feed to move on and the woman was the meanest woman I ever met meaner even than Mrs. Martin- it just took 2 days trying to trade with her but I worked on her from every angle our old friend Pick helped out with their lawyer and I sure sliped [sic] up on the blind side of her and made a good trade and will lamb there and the best lambing camp in Montana and then I will take them down to the Bad Lands just when I wanted to take them anyway as I can run them cheaper down there than rent the Fergus Ranch so it came out just as I wanted. I am going down to the sheep tomorrow and then East to Sand Springs and Edwards Post Office to see a man that I hear wants some sheep and is well equipped to run them was over to see the lambs at John Hills this evening and they are OK will be back here Monday I think and run down to see Mr. Collins and go to Billings to get 2 new tires as our rear tires are gone packing these big loads to camp. Raining a little here this evening but we have chains and can get thru just the same and glad to see the rain as that means early grass Hoping this finds you all well and happy With lots of love from Dad good night."

In the 1930's, Bair tried to sell the Martinsdale ranch. Although Charlie would deny it to his girls, he was disappointed that he had no son to carry on the ranch. Several offers were made, but no one came up with the money Bair was asking, so in 1939, he took the ranch off the market. Perhaps Marguerite's marriage to his foreman, Dave Lamb, determined his action, or the fact that his family seemed very contented living on the Musselshell.

Marguerite's husband, David Lamb.

The Depression years were tough for the sheep industry. Bair was out of the land development and oil business and concentrated on his ranch holdings and the management of his property in Billings and Los Angeles. In October of 1931, he wrote to his family, "I was over to the bank today clipping a few coupons off the bonds and checking our bank ac and found the Bair Co balance $42,800 and thought some mistake when Mr. Westbrook looked it up I found that Marguerite had transferred her savings ac to the Bair Co. of $33,000 .This was sure a surprise to me and she never said a word to me about it. I want to thank you all for your cooperation in this depression and want you to know that transferring your savings to the Bair Co is not transferring it out of your hands as I am going to show you it will all come back with interest if in my power and if times will break halfway our way but the loyalty is what affects me deeply. If can get straightened out here tomorrow may take a run up to Lewistown and get fixed up there and come to Martinsdale before going to

Iowa. Hoping this finds you all well and happy Lots of love from Dad."

Bair continued to live more quietly on the Martinsdale ranch during the last decade of his life. He was among those made an honorary Colonel in the Montana National Guard by Governor Roy Ayers.

Huffman photograph of E.E. Gray and Charlie at the Bair ranch, Martinsdale.

In 1941, the Little International Livestock Show at Montana State College dedicated their show to Bair and E.D. Dana of Cascade.

Bair's birthdays were usually noted in the state newspapers—and, more often than not, it was reported that he spent the day supervising the shearing of sheep. In a letter from Winnett shortly before his birthday in 1932, "Had a good breakfast at 5 this morning in order to get the sheep in in time to start shearing at 7 a.m. a beautiful morning and the country never looked better than it does now with all kinds of feed every place and water Had heavy rains and cloud bursts that took all our dams out down in the bad lands but we can put them in again if we get more rain. We will finish here last of the week and then shear at Forest Grove then shear at Armells the Old

Fergus ranch we have leased and will store all our wool at Lewistown for the present. got cleaned up and changed clothes and a good nights rest while in Billings and feeling fine with good feed and water every where kinder gets a fellers spirits up a little if wool isn't worth anything. Harry Mayer and Les Works may call on you last of the week as they are coming up to see the wool give them dinner if they come that way."

In another letter from the Burke Hotel in Lewistown (European plan, rates $1.00 to $3.50), he cautioned his ladies, "...if you chance to see or hear of a wool buyer by the name of Bliss if he comes over that way let me know or tell him I want to see him as he is the man I sold to year before last for 24 cents and he told me he made some money on the wool also tell Frank to get in touch with me if he shows, also Punk Ward...have the yearlings cleaned up and on their way to the Mosby country...I am anxious to get home. the Hills gave me a birthday dinner and a peach. What I mean one of the most beautiful birthday cakes you ever looked at with 75 candles on it lit up I blowed them out with one breath. Thought it awfully sweet in them at such a busy time ..."

Harry Mayer of Chicago, who bought Bair's sheep, shared the same birthday and for 20 years came to Montana to be with Bair on their birthdate.

On Bair's 85th birthday in 1942, Mary Bair and Alberta had a dinner party for him at the Grand Cafe in Billings with guests Mr. and Mrs. Harry Mayer of Chicago;

Charlie with unidentified friend.

Mr. and Mrs. George Sinton of Manhattan; Mr. and Mrs. R. E. Cooke, Bair's lawyer; Mr. and Mrs. Frank P. Mackey; Mr. and Mrs. Harry A. Snyder; and Mr. Sterling Wood, another lawyer. They were all long-time friends from the livestock industry and business. (Dave and Marguerite Lamb were at the Martinsdale ranch supervising the shearing.) It was his last birthday party.

Following World War II, the Bair family sold some of the land at Martinsdale, but then, in 1959, 1960, and 1963, Alberta and Marguerite bought more land, bringing the deeded ground back up to about 50,000 acres.

Chapter 15
MARGUERITE AND ALBERTA
The Bair "Cubs"

When the Bairs made their home in Martinsdale, Marguerite was in her early forties and Alberta in her late thirties. The change of lifestyle was abrupt for the two women, who were used to the Portland society life of bridge and golf and travel.

A friend, Grace Stone Coates of Martinsdale, wrote of the girls: "Marguerite is the Spanish type, with an angelic disposition and a voice like an angel. Alberta plays cards and golf like a man, and that is a fine compliment—if one picks the man. She has impeccable card manners, with no feminine dirt."

Henderson Coates, Grace's husband, was an excellent card player and he taught the girls how to play poker. The foursome had some good card games over the years. The girls also enjoyed hunting, and Alberta was in her eighties before she stopped driving the Cadillac up the creek to go deer hunting. She always got her game.

Charlie continued to cherish and protect his family, even as the girls became women. He expressed his concern to Mary about the girls driving from Billings to the ranch in bad weather:

"Dearest Mate Just a line it was raining when I boarded the train last night and raining when I just got through at the N.P. Land office and they treated me awfully nice on range and water for the sheep. I have just phoned the Girls but they were out I am leaving on the first train for Billings will be there at midnight as I did not want the Girls to start out not knowing how the roads were as I know they must be a fright up thru the basin and want to be with them coming home as they do not realize the hardships motoring thru the gumbo I got a good nights sleep and feel fine riding on the train is easy in comparison to pounding around on the trucks I have been riding thousands of miles. Will be home just as soon as I possibly can take good care of your self as I can do enough work for both of us with lots of love Dad"

Alberta was engaged many times, but never felt deeply committed enough to go through with marriage. Marguerite, too, had a number of engagements but didn't leave the family home, even after she married. While still living in Portland, a young man from New York fell in love with Marguerite and courted her

Huffman photograph of young Marguerite.

through the mail for several years. At his suggestion that Marguerite come east to meet his sister, Charlie countered with an invitation for them to come to visit the Bairs. Charlie didn't believe in relinquishing control of any situation. Marguerite finally ended the relationship because she couldn't make the commitment to leave the family and live in the east. The young man's life ended tragically a few years later in suicide.

The girls continued to travel to New York and Chicago and other places back East, visiting friends and shopping, enjoying the flexibility that money allowed. However, they always returned to the shelter of the family home.

At the Martinsdale ranch, Bair hired a Scotsman by the name of Dave Lamb as foreman. Lamb had been ranching on the Stillwater, but after losing his wife, he had left the ranch to his son and moved on. Lamb had the ruddy look of his Highland kin and a delightful sense of humor. For relaxation, he wrote poetry.

Marguerite was attracted to the handsome foreman and, on January 3, 1939, they went to White Sulphur Springs and were married—upsetting, the local paper related, elaborate plans for a home wedding. Marguerite had slipped her wedding clothes out of the house and changed in a sheep wagon.

The family hadn't moved to the main ranch buildings on their return to Montana, but had remodeled around the old Grant ranch home, about a mile from the headquarters. The house was ready in time for Mary and Bair to hold Open House for their fiftieth anniversary. Over the years, Alberta and Marguerite added to the house and its furnishings until there were finally 26 rooms. The old ranch house was no longer distinguishable.

It became the custom of the Bair sisters to go to the Mayo Clinic for a check-up each year and then on to New York and Europe for two or three months to shop for antiques. They shopped for antiques as they did their other business—after consultation, Marguerite would make a decision and send Alberta to negotiate the price. One year they arrived in London late in the day and were out for a walk when they saw the shutters being lowered in the antique shop across the street.

Hurrying over, they rapped on the door, and the owner politely told them the store was closed.

"Yes," said Alberta, "but was that Paul Storr silver in the window?"

The gentleman opened the door and invited the girls in. "Anyone," he said, "who could recognize the silver from across the street with the shutters coming down, should come in. I just got these in and was unpacking them."

Alberta and Marguerite told him they would come back in the morning. That evening, as they were having dinner at the Savoy, the store owner also came in for dinner.

"Oh, dear, Sissy," whispered Alberta to Marguerite, "when he sees we are staying here, we will never be able to get the price down on the silver."

But they did buy the silver, and at a good price. It seemed one of the young English lords, when in need of money, would go to one of the family estates and take some silver in to the antique shop. His family was chagrined, but since the pieces were his inheritance, they did nothing about it.

Alberta always gave Marguerite credit for the decorating and impeccable choices of antiques, but Alberta, too, was very knowledgable about the value and prices of what they bought.

As the house grew with its additions, so, too, did the idea grow to leave the house as a museum for the people of Montana.

With its artistic blend of European furniture and western artifacts, it would be a beautiful gift.

Today, while most of the house reflects a European influence, it is in the Pine Room where the presence of Charlie Bair is most felt. Pictures of Bair and Russell are on the mantle, and next to the fireplace is a picture of the train of wool that was sent to Boston in 1910. The west wall is covered with the beaded artifacts from the Crow Reservation days, and works by Sharp hang on the walls. A letter of Russell's inscribed, "If you don't hook up with C.M. Bair, return," hangs near an Indian dress decorated with elk teeth that belonged to Plenty Coups' daughter. Other photographs show Bill Hart and Will Rogers, Will James, and Plenty Coups. Alberta's toy tepee stands in a corner.

Marguerite and Alberta continued their practice of traveling to Europe each winter where they bought antiques to fill the expanding house at the ranch. During the war years, they traveled to the Caribbean. London became their favorite city for buying antiques, although they enjoyed the times spent in Italy and Spain because of the rich culture there. By 1970, they would have made twenty Atlantic crossings.

The house was one more tangible symbol of Bair's legacy.

Chapter 16
NOT THE LAST CHAPTER
The Legacy Continues

When Charles M. Bair died in March of 1943 (with his family in attendance) at the Northern Hotel in Billings of a heart ailment, letters and telegrams poured in from around the country. Services were held in the First Congregational Church. Among his active pallbearers were life-long friends: Lee Simonsen, of the Padlock Ranch; E.T. McCanna, a banker; Sterling M. Wood, Bair's lawyer for forty years; Frank Mackey, an old-time stockman; Robert Leavens, in government; and E. Phillips of Helena, the Executive Secretary of the Montana Livestock Association. More than fifty honorary pallbearers were listed. They represented the business associates, friends, and neighbors of a productive lifetime.

Most of the senders of letters and telegrams remembered something special. "Dolly" Martin wrote from Florida where she was serving in the army:

"...I have always thought of Mr. Bair as a sort of godfather. I can remember him so well when I was a kid in Forsyth—he always wore a big racoon coat in the winter time and took time to joke with me. Then again at grandfather's funeral in Billings—it was such a grown up affair, and I was sort of lost—and he took time to bother with me. And later at Martinsdale when he made it a point always to tell me when I went away to school that I should remember where home was and my friends were if ever I needed help. He was always so considerate and somehow I grew up feeling he was just like all landmarks and standbys and would always be there—sort of an 'anchor to leeward' in case I needed him. I'm sure many others feel the same loss as I. He seemed ageless."

From another friend:

"...Everyone will miss Mr. Bair. I always think of him wearing a red tie and such good looking clothes. I was glad when Helen told me that he was laid to rest in his red tie."

Bair's red ties were hand crocheted by Alberta as a Christmas gift each year.

And from a friend in Helena:

"Charles Bair was one of the best friends I ever had. I admired him tremendously. He was an outstanding citizen of the highest integrity. Probably what endeared him most to his friends was his loyalty to his friends and his wise and thoughtful counsel."

Bair changed the scene of Montana in the sixty years he had lived there, and his fortune continues to have a tremendous impact on the cultural life of Montana. He'd been the largest individual sheep owner on the continent, possibly the world. He'd been the first to drill for oil in the rich fields of Wyoming, ventured into the coal business, and spent years on the Rosebud Irrigation project. At the same time, he had interests in banks, public utilities, and a newspaper. He was active politically and took time to help the less fortunate.

All of these activities went on with Charlie's active participation. His daring venture into the Klondike paid off handsomely, and he used that base to expand and develop an empire of interests. Regardless of how well he did, he was a close observer of the economics of his businesses.

One day in Billings, Bill Trask was visiting with Bair at the Grand Hotel after Bair had loaded up a wagon with groceries and supplies for the driver to take to the herders. The wagon was filled to overflowing with groceries, brooms, and other supplies.

The driver came back to the hotel, looking the worse for wear, and told Bair he'd just gotten to the top of the Rims when the horses bolted from a snake and the wagon and horses had gone over. He was lucky to be able to jump and save his life. When there was no comment from Bair, he asked, "Wouldn't you have jumped, Mr. Bair?"

Charlie chewed on his cigar for a minute and then replied, "Well, if it had been me, with all those supplies on board, I think I might have ridden it down halfway."

Bair was a man of few words, and kept his own counsel on his business dealings. Alberta once commented to her Dad that he didn't talk much. He replied, "Toddy, when I'm talking, I'm not learning anything." He loved the excitement of negotiating a good deal as much as the money he made from it. His sense of competition heightened his innate business sense, and he had a rightful pride in his accomplishments. His family was proud of Charlie, too, although he didn't allow them to share his business life.

Nine years after Charlie's death, Mary Bair died at the age of 87, also of a heart condition. She had been in the hospital about three weeks and was planning to return to the ranch with her daughters when she died unexpectedly.

"Muzzy" to her daughters and "Aunt Mary" to the Reynolds family, Mary Bair had been a remarkable woman. She was able to make a home for her family, whether on a homestead in Lavina, in a Portland home surrounded by antiques, or wintering in southern California. She adjusted to ranch life on the Musselshell as well as she had city life in Portland. Friends and family remembered her sweet, calm disposition first, but they sooned learned that beneath the calm exterior was an intelligent, capable person with a marvelous sense of humor. Although she had no advanced education, she was able to adapt and grow as years passed.

The separation when Charlie moved his family to Portland had caused some estrangement, but Mary coped with that as well. And when it came time to move back to Montana, Mary left her comfortable home in Portland without a second thought. She loved Charlie Bair, but more importantly, she understood him. He chose to place his family in a sheltered position, giving them everything they wanted and insulating them from the life he led in the business world. Although Bair chose to include his daughters in his business later in life, Mary was always sheltered.

From the time of Mary's illness in 1934 and Charlie's bout with gall stones the following year, the Mayo Clinic would become one of the recipients of the Bair philanthropy. Mary was a supporter of many charitable organizations in the state, a charter member of the YWCA, and a supporter of the Christian Science Church. Living in Martinsdale, she took part in the local Community Aid and gave the land for the Community Hall.

Mary was laid to rest in the Billings Community Mausoleum.

The sisters continued to live quietly at Martinsdale, entertaining less after their father's death in 1943 and their mother's in 1952.

One story in circulation tells that the sisters, in order to preserve their privacy, kept hats on the settee near the front door, and when anyone knocked to "see the house" or sell them something, Alberta would appear at the door with her hat on her head. She would explain that they were sorry, they couldn't invite them in, they were just leaving.

Years later, when Alberta was chided about the story, she started to protest, then smiled and admitted her duplicity.

One exception to this subterfuge was their neighbor, Jeanette Rankin. A Montana feminist and the first woman elected to Congress, she spent her summers at the 71 Ranch (formerly the Smith Brothers, but owned then by Wellington Rankin) and would often bring her guests to "see the house." She would appear at the door and call out, "The house, the house," and her guests would be shown "the house" and its contents.

Ranch home at Martinsdale.

Dave Lamb died in 1973, leaving more of the ranch management to the sisters. They enjoyed getting out to help flag for cattle and sheep drives up the highway, checking on range conditions, and generally keeping a close watch over ranch activities. They enjoyed most the lambing season and the shearing. At a time when most of the ranchers up and down the

Musselshell Valley were going from sheep into cattle, the girls insisted that there would always be sheep on Bair's ranch.

In 1976, Marguerite slipped and broke her ankle. Slow to heal, she was in the hospital several times as a result of the injury. She was in the Deaconess Hospital in Billings with the ankle injury when she suffered a heart attack and died on December 23, 1976. Up to the end, she was more worried about leaving Alberta alone than her own fate. She had often remarked that when she died, she hoped she had never hurt anyone. Marguerite, like Mary, was a gentle person.

Alberta was devastated by the loss of the last member of her family and the sister to whom she had been so close, but her grief was never shown to the public. She continued to manage the ranch and the Bair assets, and she began the philanthropy program the sisters had planned.

An indefatigable person, Alberta has continued to enjoy her vodka (she gave up cigarettes at age 94), staying up long after many, much younger, companions have gone to bed. Charming, opinionated, and interested in current affairs, she still enjoys the banter of politics and business more than the latest in fashion or design and is quick to share a favorite story which she relates with great gusto.

In this colorful sense, as well as in her sharp business acumen and in her generous philanthropy, Alberta remains, in artist Henry Sharp's words, "A real hickory chip of the old smoked block."

With daughter Alberta at the helm, Bair's legacy moves toward the next century in Montana.

After Marguerite's death in 1976, her estate went into the Bair Foundation to begin the gift of giving planned by the sisters. Four full-ride scholarships were to be given each year in both Meagher County and Wheatland County. Large gifts went to the hospitals in both counties. The Mayo Clinic and the Christian Science Church were also beneficiaries.

Alberta began making gifts aside from the foundation. She sold the land still owned by the family in Los Angeles and built a new science building for Rocky Mountain College in Billings. She also built a gymnasium for the Boys Club of Billings, the Trauma Center at Deaconess Hospital in Billings, the Bair Clinic in Harlowton, contributed to the Mental Health

Association, and helped build the clinic in White Sulphur Springs. The remodeled Fox Theater in Billings was re-named the Alberta Bair Theater of the Performing Arts in 1987 in recognition of her generosity to them. With all these gifts, Alberta was quick to remind people that they came from the fortune her father had made in Montana. In Bozeman, the Museum of the Rockies received a large gift for the construction of the entry way and lobby for the museum addition.

Alberta received the Scriver Award at the C.M. Russell Auction of Original Western Art in Great Falls in recognition of her friendship with the late artist. She has provided substantial donations to the C. M. Russell Museum and serves on their National Advisory Board. Alberta is one of only three women to become an honorary member of the Charlie Russell Riders, a private philanthropic enterprise. The Holter Museum of Art in Helena and the J.K. Ralston Studio and ZooMontana in Billings have also been beneficiaries.

Alberta, about 1912.

Alberta, about 1985.

Charlie Bair was made a member of the Cowboy Hall of Fame and Western Heritage in Oklahoma City in 1975, and several years later, Alberta was invited to become a member of the Hall's Board of Directors. She was the only woman member at that time.

Rocky Mountain College awarded her an Honorary Doctor of Law in 1982, and in 1986, she was awarded the Philip N. Fortin Humanitarian award.

In 1988, Alberta was awarded a degree of Doctor of Humane Letters at Montana State University's commencement exercises. The presentation speech read in part, "You have enriched our state and region in the areas of education, health care, the performing arts and the preservation of our cultural heritage; as a humanitarian, you perceived the ways; as a philanthropist, you provided the means...your generosity has touched the lives of countless Montanans..."

There have been other gifts—less publicized—such as to the libraries of White Sulphur Springs and Billings, the Meagher County Historical Society, the Billings Symphony, and the Yellowstone Art Center.

As the Billings Gazette remarked on the occasion of Alberta Bair Day in Billings, "If you study the list of recipient organizations, you will notice something. All of them, in one way or another, are connected to the work of enriching and enhancing civilization and our life on earth; music, theater, art, education, mental health and medicine."

Charlie Bair loved Montana. Its grandeur and expanse fitted the man. His family has seen that Montana will receive the fortune of the Northern Pacific conductor.

RESEARCH/BIBLIOGRAPHY

Bair, Alberta, interviews (period of 1970-1990)

Bair, Charles, letters: December 8, 1911; August 5, 1909; August 16, 1911; September 28, 1932; May 3, 1933; January 21, 1911; March 25, 1933; May 13, 1933; December 15, 1912

Banks, Manuscript, Banks and Banking, Billings Public Library

Billings Gazette

Butler, Dr. W. J., March 17, 1943

Clark, Donald H., 18 Men and a Horse, Metropolitan Press, Seattle, Washington, 1949

Coates, Grace Stone, letter, March 15, 1939

Committee on Indian Affairs hearings, United States Senate, 60th Congress, 1st Session, Document 445, Washington Printing Office, 1908

Conway, Victor, interview, November, 1990

Dixon, Joseph, letters, January 1909

Forsyth Independent

Great Falls Tribune

Hart, Bill, letter, September 7, 1935

Helena City Directory

Huntington, Bill, Both Feet in the Stirrups, Western Livestock Reporter, 1959: pp. 277-279

Indreland, Dick, interview, November, 1989

Karlin, Jules, Joseph M. Dixon of Montana, Part I: Senator and Bull Moose Manager 1867-1917

Kirkpatrick, Lillian, interview, April, 1988

Lamb, David, notes

Lamb, Marguerite Bair, interviews, 1970-1976

Martin, Elda, letter, April 1, 1943

Montana Daily Record, Helena, December 19, 1903

Moore, Charlotte, letter, March, 1943

Meagher County Court House records, White Sulphur Springs

Oregon Historical Society, Portland, Oregon

Reibeth, Carolyn Reynolds, letters and interviews, September 15, 1986; July 7, 1987; November 15, 1987

Reynolds, Mike, letter, August 3, 1970

Rosebud Land and Development Company, manuscripts, Montana State Historical Library, Helena, Montana

Sanborn maps, Montana State Historical Library

Sharp, Joseph Henry, letter to Marguerite Lamb, April 24, 1943

Shephard, Russell, letter, March 19, 1943

Terrett, Pete, interview, December, 1987

Webb, Felix, interview, November, 1990

Wyoming State Archives, Museums and Historical Department, Cheyenne, Wyoming